CANADIANS AT WAR

CANADIANS AT WAR

JIM LOTZ

BISON GROUP

First published in 1990 by
Bison Books Ltd.
Kimbolton House
117A Fulham Road
London SW3 6RL

ISBN 0 86124 641 1

Printed in Hong Kong

Page 1: *The face of battle: A Canadian soldier during a night attack in France, 25 July 1944.*

Pages 2-3: *The memorial at Vimy Ridge commemorates the Canadian victory of 9 April 1917, and the 3598 killed in the battle.*

Page 2: *A Canadian paratrooper floats to earth.*

Page 3 (top): *A soldier at the reconstructed Fortress Louisbourg, Cape Breton.*

Page 3 (below): *Faces of the modern Canadian military.*

Below: *Canadian troops leave for home, Nijmegen, Netherlands, 31 May 1945.*

CONTENTS

INTRODUCTION 6

AN UNMILITARY PEOPLE 8

THE FIRST WORLD WAR
On Land 22
Into Battle – From First Ypres to Vimy Ridge 24
Vimy 42
Passchendaele and Canada's One Hundred Days 48
In the Air 68
At Sea 80

THE SPANISH CIVIL WAR 84

THE SECOND WORLD WAR 92
On Land 94
Hong Kong 100
Dieppe 104
Italy 110
D-Day and Northwest Europe 122
In the Air 136
At Sea 152

THE KOREAN WAR 162

THE PEACEFUL USES OF
CANADA'S MILITARY FORCES 172

INDEX 190

INTRODUCTION

Remembrance Day, 11 November, is celebrated as a public holiday in Canada, marking the date of the armistice that ended the First World War in 1918. Few of those who fought in that war are alive today. And the veterans of the Second World War, which ended in 1945, are aging and fading away. As they do, the memory of Canada's military history may also begin to vanish from the consciousness of Canadians. Winston Churchill devoted only 53 lines to Canada's contribution to the Allied victory in the first four volumes of his history of the Second World War. And half of those dealt with letters to Mackenzie King about Newfoundland! In 1985, *Life* magazine's special issue on the Second World War contained no mention of Canada's participation.

In talking with veterans about their experiences, it is almost axiomatic that those closest to battle are the most reluctant to talk about it. The memories of lost friends makes it too painful. To mark the 70th anniversary of the end of the First World War in 1988, two veterans put on a singularly Canadian exhibition at Halifax's Dresden Galleries. Called *Pro Patria Mori*, the works refuted the 'old lie' propounded by the Roman poet Horace that, 'It is sweet and honourable to die for the fatherland.' The images of war showed nothing sweet or honourable, for they were based on personal experiences. One artist, Robert Dietz, born in Germany, was designated 'politically unreliable' for anti-Nazi activities

and sent to the Eastern Front. He knocked out five Russian tanks, was captured by the Russians, but escaped. The other artist, Henry Orenstein, a Canadian Jew, served with the Governor General's Footguards in the Second World War.

Canada has not been involved in a war since 1953, when the Korean conflict ended. One writer called Canada 'the Peaceable Kingdom to which those weary of conflict go to escape the burden of a national destiny.' Many people fled to Canada to escape the ancient hatreds and fears in their own countries. The central building of Canada's Parliament is called the Peace Tower, and in recent years this country has gained a world-wide reputation for its peacekeeping efforts.

As an official of the Canadian War Museum said in July 1989, 'We're not a warlike country but we have a very significant military history. . . .'

Again and again, Canadians have gone enthusiastically to war in foreign lands, become hardened in combat, and shown courage, initiative and enterprise in battle. This book tells part of the story of Canadians in combat, at the sharp end of war, fighting and dying. At first the battles took place in Canada. But, beginning in 1899, Canadians went overseas to fight in foreign wars. And in recent years, this country's armed forces have put a great deal of effort into the quest for 'the moral equivalent of war' – using resources and energy in peaceful ways to enhance, rather than to destroy, life and property.

Below left: *The Peace Tower soars above Ottawa's Parliament Buildings.*

Below: *New and old uniforms at a Remembrance Day ceremony in Victoria, British Columbia.*

Right: *The Snowbird team of Tudor jets flies over the Parliament Buildings.*

Below right: *The War Memorial in Ottawa.*

Bottom: *On a dank day in November, the people of Vancouver remember their war dead.*

An
Unmilitary
People

There has never been a war of Canadian origin, nor for a
Canadian cause.
WILLIAM ARTHUR DEACON, *My Vision of Canada* (1933)

The first recorded account of Canadians in battle comes from the Norse sagas. While exploring Vinland in 1006, Norsemen attacked a group of *skrellings*, killing eight of them. The *skrellings* may have been Indian or Inuit. The word means 'barbarians' or 'weaklings' and is typical of how a 'superior' people view an 'inferior' one. Later, these people showed their mettle when they attacked the Norsemen and mortally wounded their leader.

On his second voyage to the Eastern Arctic in 1577, the English explorer Martin Frobisher attempted to seize two Inuit as hostages. They escaped his clutches, grabbed their bows, and Frobisher retreated with an arrow in his buttocks. The Inuit fled when the English sailors fired on them with arquebusses. In 1609, Samuel de Champlain impressed his Algonquin and Huron allies by killing three Iroquois chiefs with arquebusses south of Lake Champlain. When first contacted by Europeans, Canada's Indians told of their victories: Chief Donnaconna showed Cartier the scalps of his enemies in 1545. Indians sallied forth on war parties to seek revenge, or to show their courage and bravery. Skills gained in the hunt served them well when they set out after their enemies. The Haida of the West Coast had a reputation for being warlike, and their war parties brought back slaves to serve them. The native peoples of western Canada dealt in summary fashion with anyone they considered enemies. In 1770, Samuel Hearne set out with a party of Indians to travel to the Northern Ocean. In mid-July they came across five Inuit tents on the Coppermine River. Hearne describes his Indian companions as 'an undisciplined rabble' and 'by no means accustomed to war or command.' Yet they

Left: *The Viking settlement site at L'Anse-aux-Meadows, Newfoundland.*

Above: *In the encounter between the Inuit of Baffin Island and English explorers in 1577, six Inuit were killed.*

acted 'with the utmost uniformity of sentiment' in dealing with the Inuit. They painted their faces, tied down their hair or cut it short, and made themselves 'as light as possible for running.' Then they charged the sleeping enemy, and massacred over 20 men, women and children. The site of this atrocity is known today as Bloody Falls.

With traditional weapons and relatively few warriors, the native peoples of Canada had a limited capacity for killing. The introduction of two European innovations – firearms and professional armies – completely changed the balance of power in the New World and expanded the scope of war.

The fearful reputation of the Iroquois emerges from the pages of the *Jesuit Relations*, written by missionaries in the field between 1632 and 1672. Bent on converting the natives, they portrayed the Indians as bloodthirsty savages, conveniently ignoring the excesses committed by Christians during the religious wars in Europe. After their first encounter with the French, the Iroquois retreated as the newcomers explored and traded for furs. When the French could not find Indians with whom to fight or trade, they turned on each other. In Acadia, Charles de Menou d'Aulnay, the governor, attacked the fort of Charles de Saint-Etienne de La Tour, the lieutenant general, in 1645 and killed its defenders.

In 1648, the five members of the Iroquois nation attacked Huronia. The *Relations* for 1649 tell of their savagery in assaulting a Huron settlement with firearms obtained from the Dutch. Reconnoitering at night, they found a weak spot in the stockade, broke in at daylight and massacred the inhabitants. Then they moved on to Saint Louys and overwhelmed its 80 defenders, tying the survivors to stakes in cabins, then setting fire to them. In the same year, the Jesuits abandoned their mission at Sainte-Marie among the Hurons on Georgian Bay, and along the St. Lawrence the settlers farmed with their weapons handy. The Iroquois now controlled the fur trade and the routes west, squeezing the life out of Montreal and the rest of New France. In 1660, Adam Dollard des Ormeaux left Montreal to steal furs from the Indians. Successfully ambushing one group of Iroquois at Long Sault on the Ottawa, he retreated to a stockade when attacked by a larger party. With 16 companions and many native allies he put up a brave stand for eight days, but died in the final assault.

As the Iroquois struck east and west and spread terror everywhere, the French settlers petitioned Paris for professional soldiers. In 1665, the Carignan-Salières Regiment disembarked at Quebec, fresh from war with the Turks, completely unequipped, mentally and in every other way, to fight a war in the forests of North America. In January 1666, 300 regulars and 200 local militia marched into Iroquois territory, and lost a fifth of their strength. A larger expedition in September ravaged Mohawk land south of Montreal and secured peace. But the Indians, increasingly drawn into the contest between the British and French in North America, continued to raid the settlers. In 1689, the Iroquois burned

Right: *A French infantryman's finery in 1659* (above) *contrasts sharply with the practical dress of a* Canadien *soldier setting out for war in winter around 1697* (below).

farms near Lachine, and *Canadiens* and their Indian allies reciprocated by attacking Schenectady, Salmon Falls and Portland. In that year, William Phips of Massachusetts attacked settlements in Acadia, but failed to take Quebec in 1690.

Canadian-born Marie de Verchères held Indians at bay for two days in 1690 when they raided her seigneury. Two years later, when Mohawks attacked the area again, her 14-year-old daughter Madeleine held the fort (literally) until relief arrived. An illustration by C. W. Jefferys of this event shows Madeleine, dressed as a demure girl guide, saluting the leader of the soldiers who saved her.

For almost 70 years, the French and English, with their Indian allies, fought each other along the boundary between their possessions in the New World whenever war broke out between them in the Old World.

When France lost Acadia and Newfoundland in 1713 at the Treaty of Utrecht, she retained Cape Breton Island. Here arose the mighty fortress of Louisbourg, an expensive and futile essay in using eighteenth-century military methods to protect a frontier land. Its walls crumbled under the damp and cold of Cape Breton, the soldiers mutinied, and the garrison and settlers starved amid the pervasive smell of drying fish. When war broke out yet again between Britain and France in May 1744, soldiers from Louisbourg raided Canso and captured a num-

Top left: *General William Pepperell was Commander-in-Chief of the New England force of 4000 which captured Louisbourg on 16 June 1745.*

Left: *General James Murray was Governor of Canada from 1763 to 1766 after serving with James Wolfe during the siege of Quebec in 1759.*

Above: *The New Englanders in landing barges attack the fortress of Louisbourg on Cape Breton Island, Nova Scotia, March 1745.*

ber of prisoners – and a quantity of codfish. When released, the prisoners hastened to New England to tell people there of the weakness of Louisbourg. In March 1745, an army of New Englanders and a British fleet came together to reduce Louisbourg, a perpetual problem for them both. The members of the amateur army refused to obey the officers assigned to them, preferring to choose their own. A raiding party crept up on one battery. Then a drunken soldier let out a loud 'Hurrah,' alerting the garrison and costing the lives of 189 of his fellows. Nevertheless, Louisbourg fell.

In 1748 the British handed back the fortress to the French, and ten years later had to assault it again when war broke out between the two countries. On 13 September, James Wolfe led the British regulars who defeated the French militia and professionals on the Plains of Abraham at Quebec. In a final set-piece battle, the British lost 68 men and the French about 600. James Wolfe and the French commander Montcalm died heroic deaths. France had lost its empire in Canada, but the *Canadiens* retained the memory of their heroes and martyrs. Britain became the dominant power in North America and soon would have to deal with a revolution there.

As the Seven Years War ended in 1763, Pontiac, war-chief of the Ottawa, seized eight British forts, besieged others, and spread terror along the frontier. His revolt collapsed, and he was killed by his allies.

In 1775 the British faced a more serious threat as the Thirteen Colonies rebelled. The Americans attacked Quebec, the seat of British power in North America, on 31 December but failed to take it. Despite this loss, the Americans won the war, using bush ranger tactics against an army still clinging to the formal ways of the European battlefield, At the peace conference in Paris in 1783, Britain gave up her possessions on the Eastern Seaboard of North America.

In 1812 the new nation declared war on Britain as she fought Napoleon in Europe. English and French settlers and their colonial rulers came together to protect Canada from American invaders attacking through Detroit, the Niagara Peninsula, and the 'warpath of nations' – the Richelieu Valley. At Queenston Heights on 13 October, Major-General Isaac Brock rebuffed the Americans, winning a great victory but losing his life.

In the following year the Americans again failed in their attack on the Niagara Peninsula but secured control over Lake Erie after the Battle of Put-in-Bay on 10 September. Bent on grabbing the western peninsula of Upper Canada, the Americans did not concentrate on taking Montreal and cutting the British lines of supply. Their feeble attempt at a northward thrust in this area ended at the Battle of Châteauguay on 26 October 1813. Charles-Michel de Salaberry, commander of the British forces in

Above: *Visitors can step back in time at the reconstructed Fortress Louisbourg.*

Left: The Death of General Wolfe *on the Plains of Abraham, Quebec, painted in 1770 by Benjamin West.*

Lower Canada, led local militia and Indians in a minor skirmish that has become a major myth in Canadian history. The militia, officered by men from noble and seigneurial families and their sons, had little knowledge of combat. Before the battle, the men spent days chilled by autumn rain, sleeping in the woods and subsisting on fat pork, biscuits and rum. One thousand Americans tried to take de Salaberry's troops from the rear, but lost their way in the woods, and a frontal assault on the *Canadiens'* position also failed. The American commander, ordered to return to the United States for winter and deterred by de Salaberry's strong position, broke off the engagement. The Canadians had seven dead and 14 wounded.

In 1814 the Americans again went on the offensive in the Niagara Peninsula, winning some initial victories at Fort Erie and Chippewa in early July before losing the Battle of Lundy's Lane on 25 July. The defeat of Napoleon released British troops to fight in Canada. On 1 September, General Sir George Prévost led an invasion force down the Richelieu Valley. Losing a naval battle at Plattsburg, he then retreated. Meanwhile Sir John Sherbrooke, lieutenant governor of Nova Scotia, annexed Maine,

setting up a customs post at Castine whose revenues went to found Dalhousie University in Halifax.

By this time, both countries had worn themselves out in war. But for the next few decades, fear of an American invasion dominated military thinking in Canada, leading to the creation of an expensive system of defence works which illustrates a persistent theme in Canada's military planning. The forts and the canal system between Ottawa and Kingston never had to play a role in the defence of Canada, but they were good for business. Budgeted at £169,000, the canal system cost £1,134,000. It is now used for pleasure craft, and the forts have become tourist attractions.

While casting nervous glances southwards, the rulers of Canada failed to recognize the rising tensions among the new middle class in Upper and Lower Canada, and in 1837 rebellions broke out in both colonies. On 4 December, a rabble in arms marched down Yonge Street in Toronto to present its demands to Lieutenant Governor Francis Bond Head. Led by William Lyon Mackenzie, a fiery orator but an ineffective military leader, the rebels were no match for the loyal troops at Montgomery's Tavern.

Below: *The USS* Constitution *('Old Ironsides') rakes the crippled HMS* Guerriere *off Nova Scotia, 19 August 1812.*

In Lower Canada, Louis-Joseph Papineau, Speaker of the Assembly, articulated the concerns of the new educated class of French Canadians frustrated by the domination of business and government by the English. Papineau preached caution to the *Canadiens* but could not control the rising tensions which led to pitched battles between factions in the streets of Montreal in October 1837. Ineffective in turning from talk to action, the leaders of the rebellion managed to win their first battle with British soldiers at Chambly on 23 November. British bayonets routed the rebels at St. Charles on the same day, and on 14 December British artillery smashed the *patriotes* at St. Eustache and the uprising ended. When the Canadians formed their own battalion of the International Brigade during the Spanish Civil War 100 years later, they named it after the two leaders of the failed rebellions of 1837.

During the nineteenth century a militia culture arose in Canada as the British tried to shift more responsibility for defending the country onto local shoulders. In 1864, Lt. Gen. Sir William Fenwick Williams, the officer commanding British troops in Canada, complained that their presence had not made Canadians more warlike, adding that the locals seemed 'to look on their coming dangers with the eye of a child, under the protection of a Parent who is

Above: *Armed with an assortment of weapons, rebels marched down Yonge Street to attack Toronto during the 1837 Rebellion.*

Left: *Louis Riel, the visionary Métis leader and early advocate of western separatism.*

bound to fight, whilst they pursue their ordinary business, or agitate themselves by fruitless party politics and parliamentary conflicts.'

Major Charles A. Boulton would not have agreed. Born into an influential family in Upper Canada in 1841, he obtained a commission in the 100th Prince of Wales Royal Canadian Regiment by securing money from his father, hiring a bagpiper, and recruiting 20 men as his contribution to the army. After ten years in Britain, Gibraltar and Malta, he took his discharge, became a major in a militia regiment, joined a survey party in 1869 and headed for the Northwest Territories. The activities of the surveyors upset the Métis in what would become Manitoba. The Métis, the offspring of Indians and French-Canadian voyageurs, had created a unique society in the West, based on buffalo-hunting and the fur trade. Their leader, Louis Riel, stopped the surveys and occupied Fort Garry (now Winnipeg). Boulton played an active role in rallying loyal settlers

and Indians. The government sent out 'friendly commissioners,' including Colonel de Salaberry, 'for the purpose of enlightening the French half-breeds as to the good disposition of the Government towards them, and to reassure the people.' Ottawa also sent a military force under Colonel Garnet Wolseley. Riel fled, Manitoba became a province, and the restless Métis moved West to empty land where they could follow their free but disciplined way of life. But an influx of settlers and hunters began to press upon the plains and those living there. The whisky traders from Fort Benton, Montana, sold their wares to the Indians as the buffalo vanished under the guns of hunters. At Cypress Hills in Saskatchewan, American wolf hunters attacked an Assiniboine camp and killed 20 Indians in the spring of 1873. On 30 August in that year, the North West Mounted Police came into being to guard the West.

But Ottawa had failed to heed the lessons of the

Left: *Guns of 'A' Battery, Regiment of Canadian Artillery shell Batoche, North West Territories, in the final battle of the Riel Rebellion, 9 May 1885.*

Below left: *Miserable Man and other Indians surrender at Battleford, Saskatchewan, after the defeat of Riel at Batoche.*

Left: *Lt. Arthur Howard with a Gatling gun used during the Riel Rebellion.*

Above: *Soldiers on their way west to fight Riel's rebels try to sleep in one of the Canadian Pacific's day coaches.*

first Riel Rebellion. In 1884, the Métis and the Indians of Saskatchewan called back Louis Riel to lead them. He proclaimed a provisional government at Batoche, a move that split his followers. Troops set out to quash the rebellion. On 26 March 1885, they were defeated at Duck Lake by guerrillas led by Gabriel Dumont. Troops loaded a nine-pounder gun, but could not use it because a Mountie officer stood in the line of fire. The Métis lost six men, the military twelve.

Ottawa rushed soldiers west over the partially completed Canadian Pacific Railway. The army had established the Royal Military College at Kingston in 1876, but the raw Canadian troops were led by an elderly British major general, Fred Middleton. Major Boulton raised a troop of scouts and joined Middleton's expedition. At the Battle of Fish Creek on 24 April, the Métis caught the Canadians on the skyline above a coulee and picked them off with accurate rifle fire. The army counted 40 dead and wounded. On 1 May, Colonel Otter attacked an Indian camp at Cut Knife Hill, but the Indians routed him. Then Middleton, who used the telegraph to co-ordinate his campaign, attacked Riel's headquarters at Batoche with the help of artillery and Gatling guns and ended the rebellion.

During the nineteenth century, many Canadians served in the imperial forces – and sought glory in other armies. Alexander Dunn from Toronto won the Victoria Cross at the Charge of the Light Brigade at Balaclava in 1854. William Hall, a black Nova Scotian, also served in the Crimean War, and won his V.C. manning a gun at the siege of Lucknow in November 1857, keeping up its fire as his comrades died around him. About 45,000 Canadians served in the American Civil War, and Martin Delany, of Chatham, Ontario, became the first black commissioned officer in the United States. At least four Canadians died with Custer when Indians wiped out the Seventh Cavalry at Little Big Horn in 1876. And nine Canadians served with Teddy Roosevelt's 'Rough Riders' in Cuba in 1898 during the Spanish-American War.

Arthur Buies, a radical Quebec journalist, enrolled in the army of Garibaldi, the Italian liberator, in 1860 and promoted his cause when he returned to Canada in 1862. Several hundred other Quebecers went to fight for the Pope against Garibaldi in 1867-70. Most of these Papal Zouaves arrived just as the Pope gave up the struggle, but the experience shrank the stomachs, stretched the legs and broadened the minds of the volunteers, as one noted.

When the South African War broke out in October 1899, Prime Minister Wilfrid Laurier tried to keep Canada out of it. But the idea of Empire gripped many Canadians, and eventually about 8300 served with the British against the Boers. Like the Métis, the Boers used guerrilla tactics, defeating the British three times in one week in December 1899. The Canadians first went into action on 18 February

Left: *Canadian volunteers on board SS* Monterey, *chartered by Lord Strathcona, set out for the Boer War (1899-1902).*

Below left: *Sir Wilfrid Laurier, Prime Minister from 1896 to 1911, tried to keep Canada out of the Boer War, but failed.*

Below: *Mustered in Winnipeg, a contingent from Manitoba prepares to go to war in South Africa.*

1900 at the Battle of Paardeberg, losing 18 men killed and 63 wounded. In a night attack on 26 February, the Royal Canadian Regiment lost another 12 killed. Two companies did not receive the order to retire, and when morning came they found they commanded the Boer trenches. The enemy soon surrendered.

The Canadians showed a marked talent for war on the veldt. At Leliefontein on 7 November 1900, a detachment under Lt. Hamden Cockburn sacrificed itself so that Canadian gunners could save their pieces in a rearguard action. Sgt. Holland manned a machine gun and repelled the Boers. When the Colt gun jammed, he picked it up, jumped on a horse and escaped. Lt. Richard Turner, twice wounded, also held the Boers at bay, and with Cockburn and Holland received the Victoria Cross. A fourth Canadian V.C. went to Sgt. A. H. Richardson, who rescued a

wounded comrade under fire at Wolve Spruit on 5 July 1900. In the last Canadian action of the war, a harbinger of battles to come in the next century, a rearguard of the Canadian Mounted Rifles lost 17 men killed out of 21 at Boschbult on 31 March 1901.

By the time the South African War ended in May 1902, the Canadians had shown they could fight as well as the British, even if they fared badly under British command. Then came the First World War, also known as the Great War. The Canadian Corps bore the brunt of much heavy fighting on the Western Front. Heading it was former militia officer and real estate developer Arthur Currie, who emerged as an innovative leader and a first-rate general by any standards. The history of the contribution of Canadians to winning the First World War shows what brave men can do when they are led by those who care for them.

The First World War

ON LAND

Into Battle – from First Ypres to Vimy Ridge

When Britain is at war, Canada is at war; there is no distinction.

PRIME MINISTER SIR WILFRID LAURIER, (12 January 1910)

A few minutes before 11 o'clock on the morning of 11 November 1918, a German sniper sighted on a private leading a patrol across a canal in the Belgian city of Mons and took first pressure on the trigger of his rifle. He squeezed the trigger, and 256265 Private George Lawrence Price of the 28th North West Battalion, 6th Canadian Infantry Division, 2nd Canadian Division, fell dead, shot through the chest. At 11 o'clock the Armistice went into effect.

The First World War ended where it began.

Private Price, the last Canadian to die in the war, lies in Saint-Symphorien. In the same war cemetery is buried Private J. Parr of the Middlesex Regiment, the first British soldier killed when the Germans invaded Belgium on 4 August 1914. At midnight on that day, Britain declared war on Germany.

The German plan envisaged an infantry sweep through Belgium and France and the fall of Paris in a few days. The British rushed an expeditionary force to France to meet the advancing Germans. These professionals, outnumbered 20 to one, stopped the invaders at Mons, firing 15 rounds of rifle fire a minute. Then they fell back while the French rallied their troops, and held the Germans at the Battle of the Marne.

The opposing armies dug in along a 700 kilometre front between Switzerland and the sea, and trench warfare began. From time to time the Germans attacked the Allied trenches, trying to break through and roll over their lines. Again and again the Allied commanders sent their troops over the top, trying for that 'one big push' that would defeat the enemy and end the war. And so the farmland of northern France and Flanders became a vast killing ground, a mire of mud, blood, and despair.

Into this abomination of desolation, as one Canadian soldier called it, went the eager and idealistic troops from the colonies, for as one person from Ontario put it, ' . . . this is *our* war.'

Left: *Soldiers head for the trains that will take them from Toronto to Valcartier Camp, 8 September 1914.*

Above: *A recruiting rally whips up enthusiasm for war outside Toronto City Hall.*

All Canadian troops were volunteers – and only 51 percent of them had been born in Canada. When war broke out, Canadians hurried to enlist out of a sense of patriotism, a desire for glory, or the chance of a free trip to Britain because the belief was that the war would be over by Christmas. They went optimistically into battle with boots that fell apart, clothing that disintegrated, and armed with the Ross rifle, a sporting gun virtually useless in combat. Canada, suffering from a depression in 1914, geared up its entire economy to fight the war.

Canadians, relying on imperial troops for the defence of their country, believed that amateur soldiers could meet their needs. Politicians, reluctant to concede power to professionals or even to listen to them, favored the recruitment of a volunteer militia. This led to a policy of patronage and parsimony that cost many lives on the battlefields of the First World War. The Ross rifle had been adopted as the standard infantry weapon at the insistence of Sir Sam Hughes, Canada's minister of militia. A teetotal Orangeman from Ontario, Hughes had pressured Prime Minister Laurier into sending troops to South Africa. He had gone there himself, and had been sent home for indiscipline and exposing the errors of the professional soldiers. He claimed that he should have been awarded two Victoria Crosses for his conduct in South Africa. A vain, overbearing, energetic man, Hughes swung into action when war broke out, using his network of business contacts. Valcartier Camp in Quebec went up in 20 days, and on 25 September, 30,617 members of the Canadian Expeditionary Force (CEF) embarked at Quebec and sailed for England. Sam

Right: *Colonel Sam Hughes (right), who organized Canada's overseas contingents at Valcartier Camp, 13 September 1914.*

Far right: *Officers of the First Canadian Division pose in life jackets as they cross the Atlantic.*

Left: *The first photograph of Canada's first army, returning from drill at Valcartier Camp.*

Below left: *Horsepower rescues an army car on flooded Salisbury Plain as the Canadian Army copes with British weather in 1915.*

Below: *Kit inspection at Valcartier Camp, September 1914.*

Hughes wanted to command them, but his erratic ways and penchant for patronage proved too much even for Prime Minister Robert Borden, who fired him in November 1916. The Ross rifle led to his downfall. Men in battle wept as it jammed. They had to hammer the bolt back with their heels as the enemy swarmed over their trenches, and no bravery could compensate for such a faulty weapon.

But before the Canadians went into the trenches, they had to be trained. Lt. Gen. Edwin Alderson, a British veteran, led them to Salisbury Plain. Here the chalk under the thin turf turned into sticky mud as rain and wind swept over the tents of the Canadians, giving them a taste of the miseries to come on the Western Front. Morale remained high, and the men kept their sense of humour. Diving into sheep manure while on manoeuvres, they joked about 'the Battle of Sheep Shit Hill.' In contrast to the rigid, class-bound British Army, the Canadians had an open, egalitarian attitude toward the military. They also had a casual attitude toward saluting officers, and gained a reputation for indiscipline.

The soldiers showed little respect for officers who did not treat them decently. Lt. Col. Russell Boyle, a rancher and veteran of the South African War from Alberta, commanded the 10th (Calgary-Winnipeg) Battalion. On Salisbury Plain he called his men together, took off his coat, rolled up his sleeves, and informed them that he was the same as them – 'just an

O.97

ordinary private.' Four men on the boat coming over from Canada had offered to punch the hell out of him, he added, and he invited them to step up and have it out right there. No one accepted the challenge. Switching on his flashlight to read a message in the trenches in France in 1915, Boyle received a burst of machine gun fire that mortally wounded him.

On a rainy day in early February, the Canadian Division entrained for France, passing through a storm before reaching Saint-Nazaire. Here they boarded boxcars and headed for the front, 800 kilometres away. Attached to the Third Corps of the British Second Army, the Canadians settled into billets and waited to go into the line. In October 1914, the Germans had attacked Ypres in a bid to take the French Channel ports. It failed, and left the British holding the Ypres Salient, an arrow of land reaching into German-held territory. This part of Flanders – known to the troops as 'Wipers' – became the main battleground over which troops surged back and forth for four years. Here in early 1915, the Canadians filed into the trenches under the calm guidance of British soldiers who had learned to sur-

vive there. The only professionals among them, the Princess Patricia's Canadian Light Infantry, had arrived in France late in December 1914. Made up of former British and Canadian regulars, the regiment sent out a raiding party on the night of 27-28 February. In charge was Major Hamilton Gault, the Montreal millionaire who had founded the regiment. In the first three months of 1915, the Princess Pat's had 288 casualties, including Lt. Col. Francis Farquhar, the commanding officer, killed by a sniper on 20 March.

As the Canadians settled into the trenches, they learned the unvarying routine of life there. Since enemy attacks came at dawn or dusk, every soldier 'stood to' as the sun rose and set, rifle at the ready. Will R. Bird, of Amherst, Nova Scotia, served with the Royal Highlanders of Canada (Black Watch) from December 1916, to the end of the war. He left a stark account of life on the Western Front in his classic book, *Ghosts Have Warm Hands*. One day a sniper shot away his periscope. An officer wanted to know how near the enemy was, and would not believe Bird when he told him. He decided to take a quick look over the parapet. Bird shouted, 'Don't!' But he was

Above: *Canadian soldiers clean their mud-encrusted kilts in the trenches, June 1916.*

Above: *A sentry peers cautiously over the parapet of a front line trench, September 1916.*

too late. A bullet went right through the officer's head.

During the day, the soldiers slept or dozed in 'funk holes' cut in the sides of the trenches. At night they repaired the trenches, brought up rations, ammunition and supplies, went on raids, and waited for the dawn. Cold cut into them, and rations often ran short. The kilts of the Canadian Scottish regiments slashed the men's legs and froze to the ground at night. Each dawn brought the 'daily hate,' shelling by German guns, which caused two-thirds of all casualties on the Western Front.

Death came in many ways and in arbitrary fashion on the front, and men clung to lucky charms. Toronto journalist Greg Clark carried well-rubbed coins and souvenirs into the trenches, along with a pocket copy of the New Testament, a nail from a horseshoe, and a stone with a hole in it. Clark stood only a metre and a half tall. Shortly after his arrival in the trenches, a sniper's bullet ricocheted off a piece of iron, and one portion of it hit a spot just above Clark's head. As one soldier put it, Clark was 'exactly the right size for trench warfare.'

Veterans of the First World War vividly recall the mud of Flanders that stuck to their boots, puttees, and weapons. The high water table and winter rain flooded the trenches, and the artillery shells and constant movement of men churned the soil into mud of a peculiarly tenacious character. Every old soldier also remembers the 'cooties' or 'seam squirrels' – lice that made every moment miserable.

The Canadians soon gained a reputation for daring, raiding German trenches and stalking the enemy in no man's land. Cpl. J. N. Christie, an aging bear hunter from the Yukon, ambushed a German patrol, killed its members, and took their shoulder straps for identification. Then he found that two of his four men had left their rifles and pinched German ones, and asked permission to go out and get the Canadians' rifles because he was responsible for them. He received permission – and an immediate Distinguished Conduct Medal.

Another westerner, Raymond Brutinel, grasped the essence of the new kind of warfare that emerged as the armies bogged down in the trenches. He organized the 1st Canadian Motor Machine Gun Brigade to bring massed firepower and mobility to the battlefield. On 4 February 1915, King George V

inspected the Canadians before they left for France, and called Brutinel's formation 'a pretty useful unit.' But Field Marshal Kitchener dismissed the brigade as 'difficult to employ,' and claimed that it would 'throw out of balance the firepower of a division.' Brutinel's brigade did very useful work in France, and he became a skilled proponent of the use of machine guns in war.

The Canadians at the front had to battle against the prejudices of the British, who were as new to this kind of war as they were, and the banalities of their own military system. In his book, Will Bird divided non-commissioned officers and officers into two types – princes and duds. Toward the end of the war, his platoon, having been led by 14 different officers, finally had one they liked – an older, generous man. They decided that when they encountered any tough fighting, 'Granny' was to be taken to the safest place with a soldier to ensure that no harm came to him.

Left: *Sanctuary Wood on the Western Front, July 1916: No longer a wood, no longer a sanctuary.*

Below: *The detritus of war: Equipment and clothing salvaged from the battlefield, July 1916.*

Attempts by black soldiers to enlist ran into racism at the highest level. The Chief of the General Staff wrote a memorandum on the enlistment of blacks in the Canadian Expeditionary Force on 13 April 1916, stating that, 'The civilized negro is vain and imitative; in Canada he is not being impelled to enlist by a high sense of duty; in the trenches he is not likely to make a good fighter; and the average white man will not associate with him on terms of equality.' Pressure mounted for the recruitment of black soldiers, and on 5 July 1916, No. 2 Construction Battalion of the Canadian Expeditionary Force came into being in Pictou, Nova Scotia. An all-black unit, it was led and officered by whites. Sixteen black soldiers were accepted into 106th Battalion, Nova Scotia Rifles. One of them, Jerry Jones, served with the Royal Canadian Regiment in France. He wiped out a machine gun post at Vimy Ridge, and then was wounded at Passchendaele.

Canadian Indians, welcomed into the CEF, went to France with the first contingent. Pvt. Francis Pegahmagabow from Parry Island took along a medicine bag presented to him by an elder for luck. The patience of the Indians made them excellent snipers. Pegahmagabow killed 378 Germans, and also won the Military Medal and two bars for his prowess in battle. 'Ducky' Norwest, a Cree, killed 115 Germans with his sniper's rifle before falling to a German sniper on 18 August 1918.

In April 1915, Canadians moved into the Ypres Salient in double-decker London buses and filed into trenches with the French on their left and the British on their right. In front of them stretched flat

land bisected by low ridges, and six miles northeast of Ypres the high ground around Passchendaele allowed German observers to see everything that happened in their enemy's lines. One battalion took over a trench in which the hand of a dead man stuck out of the parapet. As they passed, each shook hands with the anonymous corpse. As the men dug the trenches deeper, Major 'Andy' McNaughton, an artillery officer, began to test out his scientific theories about accurate shooting, carrying a thermometer to determine the temperature of the shells. Meanwhile, the Germans made ready to try out a new and terrible weapon to wipe out the salient and the soldiers holding it.

On the glorious spring day of 22 April, German infantry huddled in their forward trenches as engineers crawled into no man's land and cut passages through the barbed wire in front of them. Hoses linked to cylinders lay over the parapets. Late in the afternoon, the enemy batteries opened fire. Then a cloud of yellow-green chlorine gas drifted towards the Canadian and French lines, followed by German infantry. Coughing and vomiting, the French troops fell back, leaving the Canadian left flank exposed. Major Norsworthy, second-in-command of the 13th (Montreal) Battalion, tried to hold the Germans back with a handful of men, but died with many of them. Four Canadian field guns broke up the mass of attackers. Frederick Fisher, a 19-year-old machine gunner from Toronto, manned his gun until killed, allowing the field battery to hitch up their horses and save the guns. Fisher, a student before the war, became the first Canadian soldier of the war to win the Victoria Cross.

And the Canadian line held.

Colonel Nasmith, an analytic chemist, recognized the gas as chlorine, and within days had found a way to counteract it. Captain Scrimger, medical officer of the 14th (Montreal) Battalion, developed an instant antidote. He ordered the men to urinate on their handkerchiefs and tie them around their mouths. This caused the chlorine to crystallize, and saved many lives.

The Canadians repulsed attack after attack with rifle fire, but by 3 p.m. about 80 percent of the Princess Pat's had been killed or wounded. When relieved, the regiment mustered only 150 men and four officers.

On 24 April, the Germans again sent gas against the Canadian lines, preceded by a heavy artillery barrage. Their infantry advanced to be met by withering fire from the 8th Battalion – 'the Little Black Devils' from Winnipeg. General Arthur Currie, a large, pear-shaped former militia officer, commanded the Canadian Brigade at the Second Battle of Ypres. He saw the Canadian Division lose a third of its strength – 6036 men – in its first taste of the kind of warfare that would characterize the Western Front for the next three years.

The British sent the 10th Battalion of Currie's brigade to take a German position near the village of Festubert on 20 May. The artillery failed to cut the wire in front of the trenches, and the men of the 10th

Left: *Sir Arthur Currie, general commanding the Canadian troops on the Western Front, and one of the Allies' best commanders.*

Battalion died in scores. Currie, noting that the attack failed, ascribed its lack of success to the absence of reconnaissance and preparation, but he was ordered to attack again on the following night. The Canadians failed to secure their objective, but did take a stretch of enemy trenches.

Then the British demanded that he attack yet again. This time, Currie gained enough time to ensure that the guns cut the barbed wire and developed a 12-point plan for the attack and its support. The 5th and 7th Battalions attacked at 2:30 a.m. on 24 May, and took their objective in half an hour. Arthur Currie became the supreme tactician of the First World War, an excellent commander who cared for his men and prepared for battle with careful reconnaissance and detailed planning. At Festubert he lost 53 officers and 1200 men, and the Canadians at the front and at home began to realize what a foul and bloody war they had entered with such enthusiasm. After each battle the wounded filtered back to dressing stations, and then came the grim task of 'battlefield clearing' – the euphemism for finding and burying the dead.

At Second Ypres and Festubert, the Canadian troops had advanced in straight lines, and been mowed down by German machine guns. A captain, mortally wounded, crawled forward on his hands and knees, shouting, 'Come on' to his men. Major George Bennett, calling out, 'Number One Company, charge!', led one assault swinging his walking stick – and died a few seconds later. A week before Ypres, a private in one battalion wrote home telling his mother to expect him soon because he was sure the Germans were beaten. Now he lay dead.

Right: *Four soldiers wearing primitive gas masks. As the photograph suggests, a range of designs of gas mask was quickly developed following the experience of Canadian and other Allied troops at the Second Battle of Ypres.*

Below: *Attacking troops had to struggle through fields of barbed wire like this, under rifle, machine gun and shell fire, to reach the enemy trenches.*

Top left: *A shell burst wounds a man of the 5th Division as he staggers down a trench in August 1916.*

Left: *Canadians in a communications trench smile for the camera, September 1916.*

Above: *A heavy howitzer – No. 1 'The Original' – in action, September 1916.*

Overleaf: *The heavy guns move to new positions in October 1916.*

If Currie learned the lessons of Ypres and Festubert, the British commanders did not. Over the winter of 1915-16, another Canadian Division came into being in England, and in February the 1st and 2nd Divisions moved back into the Ypres Salient. By then the land had been levelled and rendered desolate. Only grey, shrapnel-shredded trunks remained of green woods, and the natural drainage of the land had been destroyed so that streams flowed into the trenches. Shell holes and churned mud made bringing up supplies and any other movement hazardous.

In March, the British tried another variant of the 'big fist' approach they favoured to breach the German lines. At St. Eloi, in the south of the salient, they dug tunnels towards the enemy, installed tons of explosives at their ends, and on 27 March blew up the landscape. Then the troops advanced and took three

craters, holding on for a week, drowning when they dropped, wounded, into water. The 2nd Canadian Division moved in on 4 April to hold the line. About half of them wore steel helmets. Some of the soldiers argued about the value of 'tin hats.' But Lt. E. L. M. Burns had no doubts about them. A large chunk of shell landed on him on the Somme, denting his helmet and raising a bump on his head. Burns rose to the rank of lieutenant general, commanded the Canadian troops in Italy, and later the United Nations Emergency Force in 1954-59. He also became a strong proponent of disarmament.

At the St. Eloi craters the Canadians, bogged down in mud, could not bring up supplies and ammunition for their guns, which jammed and sank into the mire. Pounded by German artillery and swept by machine gun fire, the Canadians lost three times as many troops as the Germans, and gave up much of the ground gained by the British attack. The commander of the Canadian Corps, General Alderson, blamed for the Canadian shortcomings in the battle, was replaced by Lt. Gen. Sir Julian Byng on 29 May 1916. He saw the Canadian troops for what they were – not mere cannon fodder, but tough, intelligent soldiers who needed capable leadership.

He gave it to them, and the Canadians responded, referring to themselves as the 'Byng Boys.'

On 1 June 1916, the Canadian 1st and 3rd Divisions held the crest of Ypres Ridge as patrols and aerial photos brought evidence of a pending attack by the Germans. On the following day came a massive assault of grey-coated infantry equipped with rifles, bombs, and flamethrowers. They captured machine gun posts and overran a Canadian battery where the gunners fought to the last with their revolvers. The Princess Patricia's, now filled with men from Canadian university companies, suffered 400 casualties, including their commanding officer Lt. Col. Buller. Major Gault lost a leg.

Raymond Brutinel, now a colonel, had a leave warrant but decided to visit the Canadian Corps area. He soon became involved in the Battle of Mount Sorrel, taking the 1st Canadian Motor Machine Gun Brigade to plug a gap in the lines. Ordered to withdraw, he refused to do so. General Byng called him to his headquarters for an explanation. Brutinel provided one. So Byng ordered him back to hold the line and support the infantry. The colonel said it sounded like a good way to spend his leave. The British general asked another officer, 'What sort of fools have we got here?' He asked Brutinel if there were many officers of his kind in the Canadian Corps. Brutinel replied that most would have done as he did.

By 13 June, Canadian counterattacks had gained back most of the land lost in the salient. Then came the Battle of the Somme.

The commanders of the Allied and German armies each sought to make one great breakthrough, smashing the enemy lines and allowing the cavalry to charge forward and cut down the retreating soldiers. Instead, their soldiers moved backwards and forwards a few hundred metres, in sudden surges, at a cost of thousands of casualties. As the Western Front became stalemated, the Germans dug elaborate fortifications. Thick belts of barbed wire protected their trenches and strong points, and in deep dugouts the Germans waited for the artillery barrages to end, then swarmed into the trenches to man machine guns and sight their rifles at the waves of attacking troops.

The Newfoundland Regiment had served at Suvla Bay in Gallipoli. It arrived in France in March 1916, and went into the line on 22 April as part of the British 29th Division, facing Beaumont Hamel, a particularly strong part of the German line. On 1 July, the first day of the five-month Battle of the Somme, the Newfoundlanders went over the top, 801 strong. They did not charge over the open ground toward the enemy, for each carried 60 pounds on his back – 120 rounds of ammunition, two sandbags, two grenades, a helmet, a smoke helmet, rations, a groundsheet, and field dressing. Some also carried shovels and picks. To reach their own front lines, the Newfoundlanders had to cross 250 metres of bullet-swept ground. From there they could see the enemy lines, 550 metres ahead, and 'the Danger Tree,' shredded by shrapnel.

Above: A Canadian gunner chalks messages on 15-inch shells. Such visual 'evidence' of the good morale of the troops was a common theme of reporters' photographs with all armies.

Right: Men of the Canadian Corps go 'over the top' during the Battle of the Somme in September 1916. One man has already been hit; the battle cost Canada 24,000 casualties.

Within half an hour the battle ended for the New-foundlanders. The preliminary bombardment had blown holes in the barbed wire, and the Germans directed their machine gun fire at the men struggling through the gaps. The dead piled up, and the attack stalled. Only 68 men came out of the attack un-wounded. Every officer died or lay wounded. Few Newfoundlanders reached the enemy wire, dying there before they had a chance to kill any Germans. In all 233 Newfoundlanders died on the first day on the Somme, or later of wounds suffered that day, 386 were wounded, and 91 were missing.

The commanding officer, Lt. Col. A. L. Hadow, a British officer, reported that the attack had failed, despite training, discipline, and valour, 'because dead men can advance no further.' His brigadier ordered Hadow to collect any unwounded New-foundlanders and make a second attack. But the colonel could find none among the silent and moan-ing men in the trenches. The soldiers had carried tin triangles on their backs to identify themselves. The hot sun flashed on them as they struggled back to

their lines, making an ideal target for German snip-ers and machine gunners.

It took four days for the burial parties, working at night, to recover the dead. And on 4 July it rained heavily as the Newfoundlanders repaired their trenches. At the end of the following day a wounded man crawled toward the lines and identified himself as a Newfoundlander. He had no idea where he was. But the survivor had become fed up with lying out on the battlefield and decided to reach help either from his own people, or from the Germans.

In his *War Memoirs*, British Prime Minister Lloyd George singled out the colony for special mention. Its regiment 'took part so unyieldingly in the conflict that it used up reinforcements far quicker than they could be sent along . . . . ' After the Battle of the Somme and engagements at Monchy and Cambrai in 1917, 'its death-roll alone was more than a quarter of all the men sent from Newfoundland. Casualties had wiped out the regiment twice over.' The New-foundlanders had a reputation of being highly in-dividualistic and independent men, yet they had

Above: *Canadians share their rations with Germans captured at the Battle of Courcelette, September 1916.*

Above: *After an attack in October 1916, it's impossible to tell whether the dead are Canadians or Germans.*

gone into battle unflinching. It must have been scant comfort for survivors to hear from a British general that they had done 'better than the best.'

The Battle of the Somme dragged on until November. On the first day alone the British lost 60,000 men killed, wounded and missing. When the offensive ended, 419,654 soldiers lay dead or wounded, their blood spilled to gain a few square kilometres of muddy French soil. By that time, total British casualties had reached 1,100,000, and the war was costing the country £5 million a day. Back in the colony of Newfoundland, almost every family mourned a member lost at Beaumont Hamel. And the government established Commemoration Day on the Sunday nearest 1 July so that all would remember that day of disaster in 1916.

In Canada the lists of casualties displayed in the windows of telegraph offices in small communities and in city newspapers grew longer and longer. The war created a demand for Canadian products from shells to wheat, and the land prospered as the conflict dragged on. The value of munitions and war materials supplied by Canada reached a peak of $388,213,553 in 1917, up from $28,164 in 1914. Children were urged to dig gardens, and older boys to become 'Soldiers of the Soil' to replace lost farm labour. A recruiting poster urged women to do their part in 'upholding the Glorious Freedom of the British Empire, by encouraging our young men to assist in this, the greatest of all Emergencies.' And as the casualties on the Western Front mounted they were told to make their sons, husbands, lovers, and brothers join up, while they still retained 'the remnants of honour.' Meanwhile 30,000 women worked in munitions and another 6000 in the civil service.

As 1917 opened, the Canadian Corps prepared to attack a slight rise in France, near the border with Belgium, and to achieve a victory that would become a keystone in creating a sense of national identity.

In December 1916, Lloyd George became Prime Minister of Britain. He would write later of what Canada's contribution to winning the war involved: 'Whenever the Germans found the Canadian Corps coming into the line, they prepared for the worst.'

Vimy

No matter what the constitutional historians may say, it
was on Easter Monday, 9 April 1917 . . . that Canada
became a nation.
D. J. GOODSPEED, *The Road Past Vimy* (1969)

At the age of 88, James Buchanan summed up the assault on Vimy Ridge in which he took part 65 years earlier in one word: 'Hellish!'
The ridge, 6.4 kilometres long and 200 metres high, served as the anchor for the German Hindenberg Line on the Western Front. French and British troops had died in the thousands in attempts to take it. 'You couldn't put a shovel down, but you'd hit a corpse,' Buchanan recalled. After the earlier attacks, the Germans strengthened the ridge with three main defence lines, building dugouts, siting machine guns and stringing miles of barbed wire. It looked impregnable – and the Germans believed it was.

General Currie received orders to capture Vimy Ridge in February 1917 as the Allied commanders prepared for their spring offensive. For the first time, the four divisions of the Canadian Corps, 100,000 men, would attack together. Currie made careful plans for the assault, following his dictum of paying for victory in shells rather than in lives. Subways led up to the ridge, railways and roads went in to bring up supplies and to carry back the wounded quickly, 87 miles of telephone cable linked the Canadian positions, and casualty clearing stations were set up. Reorganized platoons strengthened the feeling that soldiers were chums, members of a team, not cogs in a military machine. The soldiers practiced the attack on the ridge on courses behind the lines that showed the location of every German position. Andy McNaughton, the Corps' counter-battery officer, pinpointed the German guns and made ready to destroy them.

Below: *Canadian reserve troops dig in on Vimy Ridge, April 1917.*

Right: *Vimy Ridge – view from a kite balloon, November 1917.*

Easter Sunday had been a pleasant day, but toward evening drizzle began to fall, and it turned to rain and sleet as the Canadian soldiers moved into the forward positions. On 9 April at 5:30 a.m. the guns opened fire, and the troops went over the top. As well as knocking out enemy strongpoints, the Canadian artillery fired gas shells to soak the enemy positions and neutralize the gunners.

One soldier recalled that the sleet, slanting down toward the enemy lines, blinded the Germans. Reaching the first defence line, the Canadians cut down the sentries and bombed the dugouts. Machine gunners and snipers opened up as the Canadians advanced on the second line. Infantrymen worked their way behind the German strongpoints and silenced the gunners, and the soldiers surged over the third line of defences. By midmorning, members of the 25th Nova Scotia Rifles had reached the ruins of Thélus village near the crest of the ridge. A fresh northwest wind rose, blowing away the smoke of the barrage and the wisps

of morning mist. The sun broke through as if to celebrate this Canadian victory. The soldiers watched the Germans scuttle down the reverse slope of the ridge, and helped them on their way with bursts of machine gun fire. The Canadians looked out over a peaceful land toward Douai, contrasting the shell-torn desolation of the wounded land behind them with the peaceful countryside of red-roofed houses, fields and trees turning green ahead. 'You could see a fly if it moved out there,' recalled James Buchanan. Snow fell as the Canadians dug in along Vimy Ridge.

The battle ended on 12 April, as soldiers from western Canada captured the 'Pimple,' a heavily defended position at the northern end of the ridge, in two hours. As the weary men of the 85th Infantry battalion came out of battle, their commanding officer, Colonel Borden, served them tea and the Red Cross handed out dry socks and cigarettes. Back in billets, the Canadians soaked their feet in tubs of hot water. A British sergeant-major opened his battery canteen and served free drinks.

Above: *A break in the battle: Canadian soldiers play cards in a shell hole.*

Top right: *The 29th Infantry Battalion goes into battle.*

Right: *Shell cases from the bombardment of Vimy Ridge.*

Left: *Canadian soldiers bring in captured German officers, April 1917.*

Below: *The price of victory: The survivors mourn the dead of Vimy.*

Right: *Mrs C S Woods, who lost eight sons in the war, represented the Silver Star mothers of Canada at the unveiling of the Vimy Ridge Memorial.*

Below: *The unveiling of the Vimy Ridge Memorial, 26 July 1936.*

The Canadian capture of Vimy Ridge proved to be the only significant Allied victory in 1917. Ten percent of the Canadian Corps became casualties, with 3598 killed in action or dying of wounds. The battle went according to Currie's plans, and he called Easter Monday 'the grandest day the Corps has ever had.' The general gave full credit for the victory to his men. A survivor ascribed the success of the attack to 'professionalism and common sense,' a rare combination in war.

A white stone monument now rises above the old shell craters on Vimy Ridge. Inscribed on it are the names of 11,000 Canadians, 'missing, presumed dead' in France, soldiers who simply vanished in the mire of war, drowned or blown to bits. The French donated 100 hectares of the old battlefield to Canada, and parts of the front line trenches have been preserved. In the tunnels and chambers in the soft chalk where the soldiers waited to go into the attack, long-dead men had carved their names – and maple leaves.

A government publicist, writing about the monument, claimed that the pylons reaching skyward 'may seem the entrance to a fair country where prevail Justice, Truth and Knowledge.' A Canadian veteran of Vimy Ridge, visiting the monument in 1987, summed up the soldier's view of this Canadian victory: 'We had to do what we did. Some died. Some didn't. That's it.'

Passchendaele and Canada's One Hundred Days

... life in the trenches forced men to know each other in a
manner that is impossible in civilian life. One got to
realize that courage is a quality which comes to the fore
unexpectedly and is often greatest when least expected.
WILL R. BIRD, *Ghosts Have Warm Hands* (1968)

Knighted in July 1917 and promoted to command the Canadian Corps, General Currie waited for the next Allied push. The very success of the Canadian Corps in taking Vimy Ridge doomed many of its members to a muddy death in its next major battle – Passchendaele.

Currie cared for his men, and the suicidal strategies of the British High Command that led to the slaughter on the Somme cried out for alternatives that did not push heavily-laden men into the fire of machine guns and German artillery. North of Vimy lay Lens, a coal-mining centre of little strategic value. The British selected it as the site of a diversion to prevent the Germans from reinforcing their northern troops. Currie made a careful reconnaissance of the ground, and recognized that two key features dominated the town – Hill 70 to the north and Sallaumines Hill to the southeast. He suggested that they be taken, and was told that the Germans would never allow Hill 70 to be taken – Scottish

troops had almost taken it two years earlier, only to be driven back by savage counterattacks. Haig, the British commander, gave permission for the Canadians to seize Hill 70, and Currie made sure he had plenty of guns to soften up the German positions and to beat off any counterattacks.

At 4:35 a.m. on 15 August, the Canadians went into battle, and by 6 a.m. had taken Hill 70. The Germans launched 35 counterattacks in the next eight days, but failed to dislodge the Canadians. Currie said it had been the 'hardest battle in which the Corps had participated,' costing 8000 casualties.

But in the next offensive, all Currie's planning and tactical sense went for nought. The Third Battle of Ypres – Passchendaele – came about because of the desperate need of the Allies for a breakthrough. It had more than a touch of fantasy to it. Haig saw the offensive rolling over the low ridge of Passchendaele and taking Zeebrugge and Ostend, two German submarine bases. At that time the U-boats had a

Above: *After the victory at Vimy, General Currie and General MacBrien supervise field practice for the next battle – Passchendaele.*

stranglehold on the supply routes to Britain and it looked as if the country would be starved out. However, very few U-boats operated out of the two Belgian ports. Haig also envisaged a scheme for an amphibious attack on the coast of Belgium, with tanks climbing seawalls and rolling over the enemy defences. Once Passchendaele fell, the cavalry would sweep forward and meet the tanks.

If Haig had learned nothing about war on the Western Front, the Germans had. At Passchendaele they built a defensive system consisting of barbed wire and concrete pillboxes, each a miniature fortress with interlocking fields of fire. In the last two weeks in July, British shells smashed into the German lines and destroyed the drainage system. The land became a quagmire, 'one vast tormented bog' into which men, horses and artillery pieces sank. The advance began on 31 July, and by early October the British had advanced only six miles – at the cost of 200,000 casualties. Haig called in Currie on 13 October, and asked him to submit plans for the cap-

ture of Passchendaele.

As usual, the Canadian general made careful preparations. On 17 October observers reconnoitred the soggy battlefield, and the impact of every artillery shell was noted. It soon became apparent that only a direct hit would knock out the German pillboxes. Currie's staff carefully co-ordinated the work of gunners and infantrymen through pooling all available information.

Currie spoke with his troops, man-to-man, as they marched to the sound of guns. Private Pat Burns of the 46th (South Saskatchewans) recalled how they fixed bayonets and presented arms for this 'wonderful leader' in perfect order, buttons polished, rifles clean. Captain Bernard Montgomery, however, found the Canadians a 'queer crowd' who lacked 'soldierly instincts' despite their magnificence in battle and their victories. Before the battle Currie arrived at Haig's headquarters, claiming that he had not received the promised number of guns. Haig demanded he substantiate the claim, and Cur-

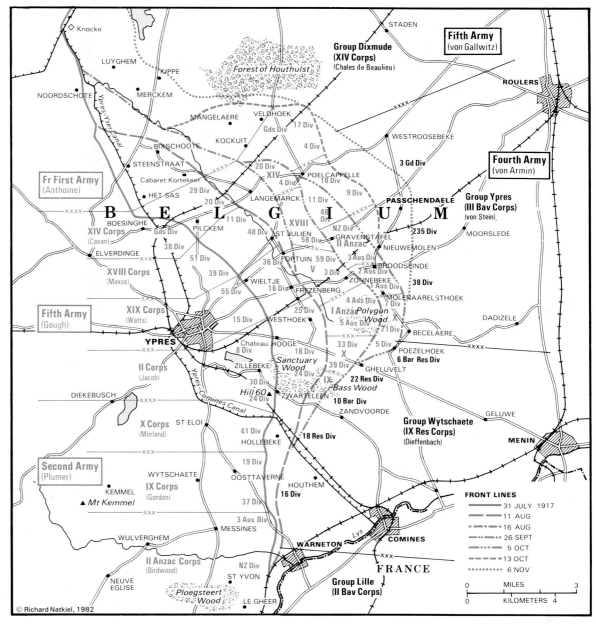

Right: *The killing fields of Flanders: The Western Front in 1917.*

rie wearily pointed out that he had just counted the guns. He got the artillery he needed. Similarly, Andy McNaughton's plans for counter-battery work were hampered by the lack of aerial reconnaissance, as German aircraft dominated the skies.

The Canadians introduced an innovation to provide firm footing in the mire, despite the derision of the British. Borrowing the idea of corduroy roads of logs used to cross the swamps of northern Ontario, they set up a sawmill and made 'duck boards' or 'bath mats.' On them troops moved to the front, and supplies came forward. The corps relied heavily on mules, but even they could make little progress in the mud. One bogged down to its belly, and began to sink further. An officer pulled out his revolver, shot the animal, then cried like a child. A lieutenant in the Canadian Grenadier Guards, blown off a plank road, began to drown in the mire. A mule clamped its teeth on his collar and saved the officer from a watery death.

The Canadians paid particular attention to providing medical aid to the wounded. At Passchendaele death lurked in the soil, tilled and fertilized with human and animal waste for centuries. Shells blew mud-saturated clothing into wounds, and gas gangrene, generated by bacteria in the soil, developed. By 1917, blood transfusion services improved the chances of the survival of wounded soldiers, each of whom carried a field dressing sewn into his uniform. The thick mud of Flanders saved many lives, for it absorbed shells and prevented shrapnel from spreading. Rifle and machine gun bullets made

clean holes, and if promptly and properly treated a soldier wounded by them could survive to fight again. Soldiers dreamed of a 'blighty,' a wound not serious enough to cripple them, but bad enough to take them out of the war forever. On his way to Passchendaele, a member of the Lewis gun section 25th (New Brunswick) Infantry saw a hospital train and predicted that he would get a nice "blighty" this time and ride on that train.' He was killed by a shell as the soldiers went over the top.

On 22 October, as Currie finalized his plans, the Canadians relieved Australians and New Zealanders who had failed to take Passchendaele Ridge. They marched away, dazed and white-faced, as if seeking their graves. A private trod on a corpse in the mud and the grunt of air that came out of the body made his hair stand on end. In that hellish place even the dead seemed to complain about the conditions. Another soldier recalled the odour of decay – 'the breath of the salient' – and the heads of dead men bobbing up and down in flooded shell holes.

The Canadians moved on to a thousand-metre-long front two kilometres southwest of Passchendaele village. This had once been a land of small villages, neat farms, pleasant meadows and woods. No trace of them remained in the ravaged land, and the swollen Ravebeck that once watered this place now flooded the Canadian positions. The men waited, cherishing their tots of rum that warmed them for a few minutes, rubbing their feet with whale oil and putting on clean socks to protect themselves against trench foot.

Left: *Tanks could smash through barbed wire, but like the soldiers, they bogged down in ever-present mud on the battlefield.*

Above: *The mud of Passchendaele. Canadian Pioneers carry 'bath mats' to provide secure footing in the ooze.*

Right: *Canadian soldiers use a shell hole to wash their feet and shave before a night attack, June 1917.*

In the early morning of 26 October, the Canadian guns opened fire while the troops waited to attack. Then came the German shells, and the liquid land wobbled and shook. Slithering and slipping, the Canadians moved toward the German positions. In their pillboxes the enemy opened up with machine guns. Many of those not killed by bullets fell wounded into the mud and drowned there. Stopped by a machine gun near a pillbox, members of the 4th (Canadian Mounted Rifles) Battalion watched as Private Tommy Holmes jumped closer and closer to it, then knocked it out with a Mills bomb. Holmes circled the pillbox and threw a grenade into the rear entrance. Nineteen Germans surrendered and Holmes won the Victoria Cross on his first day in combat. His comrades surged forward and took their objective, but only five of the battalion's 16 officers survived the attack.

A padre set out in the afternoon, a handkerchief tied to his walking stick, seeking out German and Canadian wounded. A few troops emerged, and carried the wounded men to safety. The uneasy truce lasted half an hour and saved many Canadian and German lives. But stretcher bearers knew what it meant when overworked doctors at casualty clearing stations looked at a wounded soldier and said, 'Set him down there, boys.' A burial detail would soon be taking care of him.

To the right of the Rifles, Canadians took the first line of pillboxes on Bellevue Spur. The Germans shelled the troops, then counterattacked. Lt. Shankland dispersed them with his machine gun, then went for help. Led by Capt. O'Brien, the reinforcements hit the Germans on the flank as they attacked and sent them fleeing. He and Shankland received the Victoria Cross.

Gunner Murdock MacPhee of the 36th (Howitzer) Battery described Passchendaele as 'mud, mud, mud.' If anyone fell off the duck boards, 'you didn't bother to look for them.' He recalled 70 years later how the horses would 'lay into the traces and breast collars' but be unable to move the guns out of the mud. So the gunners grabbed the drag ropes and hauled the howitzers into place to provide supporting fire for the infantry.

On 30 October, the Canadians attacked under a blood-red sky. German shell fire proved ineffective, but machine guns and rifle fire shredded the ranks. The 72nd (Seaforth Highlanders of Canada) Battalion followed a Canadian barrage and carried a strongpoint defended by 24 machine guns. Lance-Cpl. Irwin saw the crews of three German machine guns waiting to fire at the advancing Canadians at point blank range. He slid in behind them and wiped them out with his Lewis gun.

The Princess Pat's had to cross 2000 metres of slime to reach their objective, with German snipers picking them off as they slithered forward. Within an hour every officer had been killed or wounded.

Major Talbot Papineau left a safe staff job to return to the front. He wrote to a friend that since he volunteered 'life has seemed like the ball in a game of roulette trembling uncertain upon the edge of either

Beginning or End.' He saw no heroism, no glorification, no reward in war. On the night before his regiment, the Princess Pat's, went into battle, Papineau wrote to his mother, saying that they had been 'fortunate so far and all things are cheerful.' He had enjoyed the box of candy that his mother had sent, adding that, 'There seems so little to say when if only I knew what was to happen I might want to say much more.' The major died in a shell burst as his regiment attacked. Before he went in, he had turned to another officer and said, 'You know, Hughie, this is suicide.'

At their intermediate objective only 40 men remained, under the wounded company sergeant major. More men fell, and the regiment reached a pillbox on a ridge that had not been touched by artillery fire. Then three former members of the regiment, Lt. J. M. Christie, Sgt. Mullin and Lt. Hugh MacKenzie, appeared. Christie scrambled through the mud and brought the pillbox and the supporting snipers under fire. MacKenzie moved from shell hole to shell hole, organizing an attack on the pillbox. Leading the men, he rushed up the slope toward it and died in a hail of machine gun bullets. Mullin destroyed a sniper's post with bombs, then crawled on top of the pillbox and killed its two machine gunners with his revolver. Ducking into an entrance to the post, he forced its garrison to surrender. Bullets shredded his clothing, but he remained unwounded, and received the Victoria Cross for his feat. Lt. MacKenzie received a posthumous award of the V.C. for his courage.

Above: The YMCA offers Canadian soldiers a break from battle at a canteen in a ruined building.

Top right: Men of the 22nd Battalion rest in a shell hole on their way to the front in September 1917.

Right: Canada's soldiers, now hard professionals, relax amid the mud near a free coffee stall in March 1917.

The Princess Pat's held the ridge for 36 hours under fire, beating off three German counterattacks. When they left the Ypres Salient on 20 November, 750 of their dead lay behind them.

The 49th (Edmonton Regiment) Battalion lost 443 officers and men out of 588 at Passchendaele. 'Hoodoo' Kinross, a disaster on parade but a treasure in battle, outflanked a machine gun post holding up its attack, killed the gunners, and won the V.C.. Major George Pearkes received a bad shrapnel wound in the thigh but led his men to their objective which they took at bayonet point. He won the V.C. but claimed modestly that 'he felt no more heroic than anybody else after it was all over.' The 5th Canadian Mounted Rifles lost two thirds of its strength in the attack.

What made men fight so well against such odds? As one put it about the shelling, 'You just got kind of stupified and went on with your work and never noticed anything.' An infantryman recalled a friend who took a stray bullet through the neck, and on recovery was 'offered a chance to return to the trench fellowship.' The man lost a leg at Passchendaele, but this sense of comradeship, shared peril, and deep concern for the fate of others appears again and again in the talk of veterans.

One famous photograph of Passchendaele shows a machine gun in a shell hole. Huddling into his greatcoat, keeping his head down, the soldier manning it looks up at the camera, capturing his image for all time. The man was 790913 Private Ronald Le Brun, 16th Machine Gun Company, Canadian Machine Gun Corps, 4th Canadian Division. After the German attack on his position, only Le Brun remained alive. A bullet took his buddy Toomes in the head, and blood, brains, bits of skull, and lumps of hair spattered over Le Brun's greatcoat and gas mask. 'It was a terrible feeling to be the only one left,' he recalled.

Arthur Hickson of the 25th (New Brunswick) Infantry recalled going in with the attack on 6 November. As the guns roared, a bottle of rum passed down the line of troops, and Cpl. Smokey paused to light a cigarette for what Hickson called 'the nonchalant stroll through enemy lines.' At 6 a.m. the regiment jumped off as shells threw up blankets of mud. They soon met their first prisoners – scruffy-looking men carrying a gas mask and ration bag. Light rain fell and a weak sun appeared. As they approached the ridge, four of the five company officers fell. A sergeant, shot in both legs by machine gun bullets, used his rifle to ease himself forward. The Canadians dropped into shell holes, firing at anything that appeared on the low ridge ahead of

Below: The hell they called Passchendaele. A tank lies disabled and a railway track ends in a shell hole on the battlefield, November 1917.

them. Some started to connect shell holes and build a parapet. Hickson had a bottle of rum with him, and threw it to the wounded sergeant. He took a swig and sent it back to him – much to Hickson's surprise! Some instinct warned Hickson, who ducked just in time to avoid a sniper's bullet. He saw the sniper who immediately took cover – 'it looked more like a dive than a fall.'

The Canadians finally captured and secured Passchendaele Ridge. Hickson, asked to fix a jammed German machine gun, wandered over to the place indicated but found only Canadians and Germans together in death. He had a jar of home-made jam in his haversack, but a shell splinter smashed it, mixing the contents with his spare socks. So Hickson shared a tin of baked beans with a friend as they were relieved. Of the mud, he recalled that it could not be shaken off a shovel – it had to be dragged off with an entrenching tool. And Hickson echoed the words of Marlborough, the British general who fought in this area in the seventeenth century: 'In Flanders the troops swore horribly.' With his companions, Hickson left the ridge and began the 'long, muddy, weary slip and slide out.'

Canadian veterans, even in their eighties, have sharp memories of life in the trenches. But of the fog of battle they recall only isolated incidents, con-

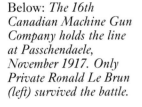

Below: *The 16th Canadian Machine Gun Company holds the line at Passchendaele, November 1917. Only Private Ronald Le Brun (left) survived the battle.*

fusion, and a lack of fear. More than any other battle, Passchendaele exemplifies the horror, bravery and futility of the war on the Western Front.

In his account of Passchendaele, Will R. Bird recalls digging in on dry ground, cutting places in the trench sides, hanging groundsheets and boiling water for 'wonderful' tea that took the chill off the night air. The men they relieved seemed to be half drunk. As they drank their tea, they heard a moaning in the mud before them. At Vimy a sentry had heard the sound of suffering, gone over the parapet and been shot by a German who had used a trick to lure him out of the trench. The sergeant ordered Bird and some others to investigate. They located a badly wounded German who snarled at them like an animal. A stretcher party carried the man back to a dressing station in a pillbox full of wounded, and laid him alongside a wounded Canadian officer. A shell landed between them, killing both men.

Bird went on patrol with an officer whose men had reported seeing some Germans in front of their position. Flares went up as they slid through the mud, and the two soldiers froze as they saw a line of enemy helmets. They crept forward, and found Germans in a rifle pit, every one of them dead from overhead shrapnel and beginning to decompose.

The platoon sat in the shell holes all day, dozing,

waiting for relief. Then an officer came into the trench, and called the men together. As Bird put it, 'His manner, and breath, told me the worst.' They had been ordered to capture a pillbox. Every man in the platoon knew two things – that the officer had no clear idea where the pillbox lay, and that he had had too much rum. The platoon commander, McIntyre, thought the strongpoint was 150 meters up the road and to the left. The sergeant claimed it was twice the distance, and to the right. No one knew the lay of the land or the location of the German defences, and half the men, including the officers, had never been in an attack. Before they went forward a friend of Bird's shook his hand – he was convinced that he would be killed, and was. Four Germans rose as they advanced and fired at the party. A bullet creased the skull of one man who went temporarily insane. Bird

and another man held him down, and Bird threw grenades into the German position, silencing it.

Suddenly machine guns opened up, and the Canadians called for mortar fire. One shell landed near Bird, knocking him out. He heard McIntyre shout 'Five rounds rapid!' and then two Germans, puffing and grunting, floundered past him in the mud. Bird pulled the pin from a grenade, counted to two, then flung it at the men who were setting up a machine gun ten metres away. Making sure that both Germans were dead, Bird heard a man calling. He found a soldier from another company with his left hand dangling from a strip of skin. All his group had become lost, most killed or wounded. Bird cut the skin with his trench knife and bound up the stump, making a torniquet with one of the man's puttees to stop the bleeding.

Above: *Shells go up to the guns on a Canadian narrow-gauge railway running through a village shattered by shellfire, September 1917.*

Then a sergeant rushed forward, reeling and shouting 'Let's give them hell!' The Germans shot him dead. A soldier came over and told Bird that McIntyre had been shot through the stomach, and lay dying. He wanted to find a stretcher and bring out the officer who had come up through the ranks, and was popular with the men.

Bird moved forward to the limit of the platoon's advance – about 100 metres from the jumping-off place. Here three men lay pinned down by a machine-gun, at which they could only take potshots with their rifles. Bird and another man silenced the gun with bombs. Then he looked around and saw the dead bodies of his comrades. The soldiers withdrew, taking their officer with them.

Further on, a stretcher bearer stooped over a prone soldier. Bird and his companions called to him, advising the man to drop into a ditch. He paid no attention and went on bandaging the wounded man. A sniper fired, killing him, and continued to pump bullets into the stretcher bearer's body. Bird and two companions crept back to a spot where they could see the sniper's rifle flashes, and all three fired at the German, silencing him. One of Bird's companions had reached the limits of his endurance and they had to let him rest, so it took an hour to reach the trenches, where Bird lost consciousness and lay as if in a coma till late next morning. He smelt the acrid reek of explosives, and looked out over the battlefield. In one scummy pond hands reached up, in another a knee stuck out of the filthy water. Nearby in the trench a soldier stood rigidly, feet braced, split up the middle by concussion. A dead German lay on a bank, and another body seemed to

be reclining on one elbow. A shell fell near it, and the corpse sailed into the air, appearing to salute his enemies.

The attack on the pillbox had failed. One party reached it, but the officer commanding it had been killed and his men retreated. The soldiers had their soaked, muddy kilts replaced with trousers, a draft of new men came up and filled the ranks and the 42nd were ordered into Passchendaele again. The Germans began to shell their positions with 'whizz-bangs' as they dug in. A man near Bird and a friend straightened up to say something. A shell sliced off the top of his head. As they dug shelter from the shelling, orders came to move to a new line as the Germans continued to shell and machine gun them. Bird saw a body, and asked a companion to help him haul it over and build it into the parapet. The man refused and Bird seized the corpse just as a salvo of shells fell nearby. None of the fragments touched him, but his companion, who had begun to dig in ten meters away, fell dead. A Company Sergeant Major who had been in the line for a long time had decided to make one more trip to the front before going back to base for a rest. Shrapnel tore away his jaw, and he died.

A shepherd boy, so covered in mud that Bird could not identify his unit, tumbled into Bird's pit. He kept saying something in a high-pitched voice, telling Bird that he was counting shells the same way he had once counted sheep in England. The Canadian remembered that way of tallying sheep long after the war. A new man came into Bird's shelter. He had lost his helmet and rifle, and his body shook as he made animal noises, before crawling

Right: *Members of the Imperial Munitions Board inspect shells at the Canadian Cartridge Company, Hamilton, Ontario. Women did the hard and dangerous work of filling the shells with explosives.*

away on his hands and knees. Bird looked at the watch on the arm of a dead soldier, and noted that it still ran and recorded the time as one o'clock: 'Each hour had grown to be a grim possession, something held precariously.'

Shortly thereafter, a shell landed in front of Bird's trench, burying him in two metres of earth with two companions. He heard one soldier tell others that there was no point in digging out the buried men as they were undoubtedly dead. But his companions recovered one man alive, and kept digging. A spade touched Bird's foot, and he wiggled a toe. The man below him had smothered. He had recently recovered a pair of boots from a corpse, and one of the soldiers had advised him against taking them. Now he saw that act as the cause of his death. Just before being buried, Bird and his companions had gone to assist men at a Lewis gun post hit by a shell. They had taken the gun and three Lee Enfield rifles back with them, and stacked them in their shelter. The rifles, with the bayonets fixed, had kept an air passage open that enabled Bird to breathe.

As darkness fell, Bird and a friend saw a German patrol. An officer and a company of the Black Watch arrived, and Bird told him what they were watching. He asked Bird and his companion to give him a hand in attacking them. The other man refused, but some 'quirk of pride' made Bird join the British troops. The Germans thought they were their own men, and advanced toward them. The Black Watch officer shot their leader and demanded their surrender. Bird flourished his bayonet, and one of the Germans charged at him, tripped over the body of his leader, and fell on the cold steel. The Black Watch officer had fallen over, and Bird had saved his life. The man

took out a book and made a note of Bird's name and number, assuring him of a suitable award – which the Canadian never did receive.

After holding another dying friend in his arms, Bird came out of the line. He staggered into a tent, and pitched into a crater filled with mud and stagnant water. His company had been reduced to a handful of men. Two days later the survivors, shaved and clean, formed up again. But, as Bird put it, no man who endured Passchendaele would ever be the same again, and would 'forever be a stranger to himself.' As one soldier put it, 'We had won the ridge, but lost the battalion.' Currie had forecast that the battle would cost 16,000 casualties. The total Canadian losses came to 15,654.

In Canada the flow of volunteers began to dry up as the true horror of the battlefields became known. The heavy casualties at Vimy Ridge led Prime Minister Sir Robert Borden to contemplate conscription. The following figures for enlistments and casualties in 1917 show the grim arithmetic of war and the waning enthusiasm at home:

Month	Enlistments	Casualties
January	9194	4396
February	6809	1250
March	6640	6161
April	5530	13,477
May	6407	13,457
June	6348	7931
July	3882	7906
August	3117	13,232
September	3588	10,990
October	4884	5929
November	4019	30,741
December	3921	7476

Right: In 1917, the Canadian government launched a propaganda campaign to support conscription as an election loomed.

Below: Prime Minister Sir Robert Borden chats with a wounded man at a base hospital on the Western Front, March 1917.

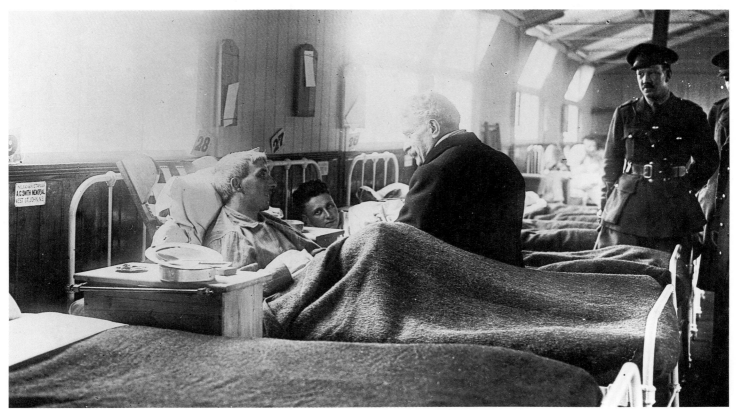

Right: *Canada, representing the Union government, points an accusing finger at Sir Wilfrid Laurier, who opposed conscription.*

THIS IS NO TIME FOR PARTY

VOTE · UNION · GOVERNMENT

On 11 June Prime Minister Borden introduced the Military Services Bill into Parliament. It made all males between 18 and 45 eligible for military service, and became law on 26 September 1917. In the following month, Conservatives and Liberals came together to form a Union government and it won a decisive victory at the polls on 17 December, with soldiers voting overwhelmingly for it – and for conscription. The government had passed the War Time Election Act on 14 September, giving the vote to the wives, sisters, mothers and daughters of serving soldiers and taking it away from those of enemy birth and conscientious objectors.

Quebec turned its back on the Union government, returning 62 Liberals, with the civilians opposing the government by 240,504 votes to 61,808. From the beginning of the war the people of the province had felt no desire to rush to the aid of France, a country that had abandoned their ancestors. But many Quebecois served in the Canadian Army, and one regiment, the 22nd – the Van Doos – distinguished itself. The case of Georges Vanier, born of an Irish mother and a Quebecois father, illustrates the difference between the intellectuals and idealists who officered the Canadian Army and the soldiers like Will Bird.

Georges Vanier studied at Loyola College in Montreal, where he was born, and then took law at Laval University and joined a firm of advocates. On 24 September 1914, an open letter addressed to Prime Minister Borden appeared in the press from Colonel Mignault, medical officer of the 65th Cara-biniers Mont-Royal, asking for authority to recruit a regiment composed exclusively of Canadians of French descent. Georges Vanier attended a meeting to bring the 22nd French-Canadian Battalion into being. He joined the new unit as a lieutenant in November. His biographer describes the future governor-general of Canada as being like 'a poet strayed into uniform.' In France he identified his reasons for going to war, noting that he could not read the accounts of Belgian suffering 'without feel-ing a deep compassion' and a desire to right 'the hei-nous wrong done.' Vanier wrote of his regiment's departure for Amherst (Will Bird's home town) to his mother in words that recall those of the early English war poets: 'It is a privilege . . . to be of this age, when instead of leading mediocre, colorless lives we can forget the dollars and the earth and think of principles and the stars.'

Left: Canadian soldiers eat their rations outside a 'funk hole' in a dry, well-made trench. A companion keeps an eye on the enemy through a periscope. February, 1918.

Arriving in France, the regiment entrained for the front, the officers travelling in second-class railway carriages and the men packed into wagons without seats or lights. At Boulogne the 'Van Doos' received the nickname 'petits cochons' from the local people, who mistook the beaver on their cap badges for a pig.

Vanier went on his first patrol on 4 October 1915, writing home to tell his family that 'the danger is not so great as you might think.' Being under fire 'is stirring; the imagination is seized, the nerves remain very firm, and you keep your head,' he added.

While Will Bird scrounged for food, and found himself one of seven men on a loaf, Vanier's batman prepared hot coffee, bovril or cocoa for him when he came into his dugout, and the officer dined on gelatine of pheasant, veal and rice, vegetable soup and mutton cutlets. If Bird or his fellow soldiers saw a piece of hardtack in the mud, they would seize it, clean it as best they could and eat it. In his first days at the front Bird found the dugouts reeking of stale sweat, 'the sour, alkaline smell of clothing,' and like his fellows spent his time searing the seams of his shirt with a candle to rid himself of lice. Vanier sat reading Shelley and the *Imitation of Christ*, writing his diary or letters home and watching other officers playing bridge.

On 9 January, Vanier attended Mass as the heavy artillery sent shells into the German lines, contrasting the symbol of charity before him and the symbol of hate and destruction above him. The death of his friend Adrian, who had the 'cleanest mind and the best heart of any youth I ever met' shocked Vanier in mid-January. Despite whatever separated the two Canadians socially, they shared a deep love for their comrades in battle and grief when they died.

On 21 March, Georges Vanier took over 'A' Company after its commander suffered an eye wound. A few months later he moved out of his dugout as the German artillery opened up. A shell hit it on the next day. On 9 June another shell exploded near him, knocking him unconscious. Fortunately it landed in soft ground, or the shrapnel would have killed him.

Sent to hospital, Vanier went back to England at the end of June, securing six weeks sick leave. Will Bird and his fellows constantly groused about their lack of leave, and the amount that officers received. Vanier was not with the Van Doos at Courcelette on 15 September 1916. The Canadian Corps, assisted by seven tanks, took the trenches in front of that village. In the evening the Nova Scotia Rifles went in with the bayonet and cleared Courcelette in ten minutes. The commanding officer of the Van Doos wrote that, 'If hell is as bad as what I have seen in Courcelette, I would not wish my worst enemy to go there.' The capture of the village cost his regiment seven officers dead, and 11 seriously wounded. When Vanier returned to the 22nd, he noted that it was necessary 'not to be downhearted' so the soldiers would concentrate on the present and the living, not on the past and the dead. Promoted temporary major, Vanier became the regimental adju-

Left: As the Canadians swept forward east of Arras in the summer of 1918, they captured hundreds of Germans, here seen in a prisoner of war cage.

tant. Here he had to deal with a persistent bureaucratic problem: a demand for acknowledgement of the receipt of some fur hats which had not been requested and had never arrived. The Commanding Officer and the adjutant decided that the hats had been 'destroyed by enemy action.' Bird tells of a soldier being ordered to cross a dangerous battlefield merely to report the number of his rifle.

The Van Doos also fought at Vimy Ridge and Hill 70, and lost 90 officers and men when it relieved forward units at Passchendaele.

Georges Vanier's war ended at Chérisy, near Arras, during the final drive across Flanders that ended the war. At 10:03 on the morning of 26 August 1918, the Van Doos left their trenches and began to move from shell hole to shell hole toward the German lines. Colonel Dubuc went forward to reconnoitre and received a bullet through the head, losing an eye, and the regiment soon lost half its effectives. The command passed to another officer who also fell wounded. The attack ended at 5:45 p.m., with Georges Vanier in command of the regiment. The Van Doos attacked again and German machine guns ripped through them as Vanier strode forward, a tall target at the centre of the battalion. A bullet hit him, passing through his right side and splitting two ribs. A shell landed near him while the wound was being dressed, killing the stretcher bearer and peppering Vanier's legs with shrapnel. At the Casualty Clearing Station a doctor removed the officer's right leg. A severe hemorrhage brought him back to the operating room where a direct blood transfusion from a donor saved his life. Evacuated to a hospital in London to recover, Vanier wrote to his mother to reassure her that, 'The loss of the leg does not affect one in the least.' On 11 November, the day the war ended, he had another operation on his leg.

Will Bird took part in the last battle of the war, in Mons. His war had continued after leaving the mud of Passchendaele. The ground taken by the Canadians at such cost had been recaptured on 16 April 1918, as German troops surged forward in what became known as 'The Kaiser's Battle.' While the Canadians had been taking Passchendaele, the Russian Bolsheviks seized power. The new rulers negotiated with the Germans to take their country out of the war. Germany moved its troops west. On 21 March 1918, 64 German divisions attacked in Flanders, using new tactics. Battle-seasoned storm troops went forward in small groups, seeking out weak spots in the Allied lines and bypassing strongly-held positions. At one point the Germans penetrated 40 kilometres into the Allied front, and then slowed down on 5 April, giving time for the troops to dig in.

General Currie saw his divisions taken away from the Canadian Corps to shore up the British line. He issued an address to his troops, telling them of the British defeat, and commanding them to 'fight . . . with all your strength, with all your determination, with all your tranquil courage.' He noted that 'Our Motor Machine Gun Brigade has already played a most gallant part . . . . ' Since the brigade

Left: *Brigadier-General 'Andy' McNaughton (fourth from left), Canada's foremost gunner, stands to the left of General Sir Arthur Currie in this 1918 photo.*

operated in a self-contained manner, it had a great deal of flexibility, fighting independently and often dismounted. On 24 March, two batteries covered the retreat of British troops at a stream crossing. With one officer mortally wounded and many other casualties, the batteries retreated and held the line. Then the eight survivors of the 50 men in one battery escaped in the remaining car. On the following day, two Canadian armoured cars and six scouts on motorcycles encountered many exhausted Germans who had just crossed the Somme near Cizancourt. Catching the enemy by surprise, the Canadians opened up with machine guns, killing many and dispersing the rest without suffering any losses.

One captain arrived at a British Ordnance depot as the major in charge prepared to abandon it, and asked for six machine guns and ammunition. The major demanded his authority. The Canadian called his men around him, pulled out his revolver and told the British officer that it was his authority The major threatened to put him under arrest, and the captain told him he would not be able to do so if he was dead. He got what he needed and went back to fighting a rear guard action while the British withdrew to a safer place.

The Germans kept attacking through the spring and summer of 1918. Currie managed to bring his divisions together again, while Haig fumed that 'some people in Canada regard themselves as 'Allies' rather than as fellow citizens of the Empire.' On 2 July 1918, Prime Minister Borden inspected the Canadian Corps near Arras. In *Generals Die in Bed*, Charles Yale Harrison tells how the Canadians looted that empty city. When the Prime Minister addressed the men, some shouted 'What about leave?' Hamilton writes of men at the end of their tether, exhausted, pale from lack of sleep, hungry, their sodden clothes clinging to them as they marched towards the sound of guns.

Below: *Lt-Col Moshier, Capt Grant, and Capt Turnbull of the 11th Field Ambulance unit outside a captured German dug-out in August 1918.*

Their leader, General Currie, concerned always about the mounting toll of casualties, did all he could to back and support his troops. He increased the number of machine guns in the Corps, developed effective intelligence systems for pooling information, and obtained more mechanical transport and artillery. The Canadians established separate engineering brigades instead of using these specialists as infantry in the traditional manner. The innovation was copied by the British. On his visit to the troops, Borden, impressed with their physique, spirit and morale, wrote to Currie telling the general that the people of Canada were behind him to the end: 'They understand . . . that no indecisive result can repay the nation's sorrow and sacrifice.'

As the Allies prepared their summer offensive, Canadian troops stood at the cutting edge of the wave of assaults that would end the war. On 8 August began Canada's Hundred Days – the final push. In great secrecy Currie moved his divisions south to face the German lines before Amiens. Colonel McNaughton carefully worked out targets and ranges for the 646 guns covering the advance of the

Canadian Corps. Gunner Murdock MacPhee describes the shelling at Amiens as 'the only bit of strategy that was planned. We did not have to register our guns to check whether we were hitting the target. It was all laid out for us on the map, along with the ranges.' Sixty years after the event, the gunner recalled it as 'a pretty damn skillful shoot.'

On the night of 7 August the Canadian troops moved into the line. The code word, 'Llandovery Castle,' referred to the sinking of a Canadian hospital ship in the channel by a German submarine on 27 June. The U-boat then machine-gunned the survivors, and 234 Canadians died, including 14 nursing sisters. Before the attack on Amiens, a general addressed Charles Harrison and his fellow soldiers, telling them that 'two can play that game.' Then the colonel spoke, saying that he could not order them not to take prisoners, but adding that 'if you take any we'll have to feed 'em out of your rations.' All life seemed suspended as the men waited to attack. In these last few months of the war, human viciousness on both sides reached a peak. Harrison's comrades discussed how best to kill the enemy and to avoid taking prisoners. One man suggested patting the captured man on the back, then slipping a bomb in his pocket: 'I did that to a Fritz at Vimy. He just came apart.'

Their ears bleeding from the force and fury of the artillery barrage, Harrison and the others advanced. In one place the Germans had been unable even to remove the muzzle caps from their guns before being wiped out. The Canadians found the first and second line of trenches empty, then saw hundreds of Germans advancing to surrender. Some threw themselves into a shell hole and begged for mercy. The Canadians fired into the huddled mass. The tanks advanced, and machine guns opened up. And the attack rolled on. A regimental history refers to 'the black day of the German army' as progressing with something 'approaching the clock-like precision of a well-rehearsed manoeuvre.' One battalion captured a regimental headquarters at Marcelcave and found the general's porridge still warm on the table. Sgts. Murray and Sample took a dugout after firing one shot into it. Thirteen Germans emerged, and then both soldiers discovered that they held empty weapons. Corporal Good led three other soldiers in a wild bayonet charge against a battery of enemy guns, and won the V.C.

The three Canadian divisions advanced eight miles on 8 August, suffering 3868 casualties, including a thousand dead. The attacks on the following day became disjointed and uncoordinated. The Sixth Brigade, known as the 'Iron Sixth,' lost hundreds of men attacking Rosières-en-Santerre, and had to take the village house by house. Lt. Jean Brillant won the V.C. for attacking German strongpoints and a field gun, but died of his wounds. The London press hailed the taking of Amiens as a *British* victory. Between 8 and 20 August, the Canadians suffered 11,882 casualties. Open warfare had finally begun, and the ratio of killed to wounded was one to six, compared to an average of one to four in the

Left: *A Canadian soldier comforts a wounded child near Mons as the child's father looks on. The mother was killed by a shell, as the war ended in November 1918.*

Below: *General Currie leads his troops into Germany and towards the Rhine in December 1918.*

Above: *The Canadian Light Horse crosses the Rhine over the bridge at Bonn and passes the saluting post in December 1918.*

trenches. French Marshal Foch saw the Canadians as 'the ram with which we will break up the last line of the German army.' A captured German officer reported that his men refused to fight when they found they faced Canadians. He shot five of them to convince the others to change their minds.

The Canadians attacked again on 23 August, then smashed through the Drocourt-Quéant Line, a system of pillboxes and strongpoints interlaced with barbed wire and interlocking fields of fire. Tanks worked with infantry. Lance-Cpl. William Metcalf guided a tank toward an enemy trench where machine guns held up the Canadian advance, and won the V.C. The Canadians fought their way into Cagnicourt, taking a thousand prisoners. In one place, a German commander refused to surrender. His men shot him, and joined the stream of prisoners. The Canadian Corps suffered 5622 casualties taking the D-Q Line, and then faced another formidable barrier – the unfinished Canal du Nord.

On 27 September, the Canadian guns roared again, and Currie's troops moved over a dry section of the canal that he had identified as the best crossing point. The village of Bourlon fell, as did Bourlon Wood – 'seven hundred acres of oak trees, shattered, somber and accursed,' in the words of one regimental history. The Canadian Corps moved on towards the vital transportation centre of Cambrai, suffering 2089 casualties on 29 September. By 9 October, the Canadians stood in Cambrai, a ruined

city fired by the retreating Germans. Beyond the city, the Canadian Light Horse leading the advance lost a dozen men and 47 horses attacking machine guns. The Canadian Fourth Cavalry Brigade harassed the German rearguard, and took 200 prisoners after charging Gattiny Wood.

And still the Germans fought. Douai fell, then Valenciennes, and in the last four days of the war the Canadians advanced four miles. A strange silence came over the battlefield on 10 November, and 'there was a feeling . . . that things were going to end . . . .' recalled Gunner MacPhee. 'It didn't seem very dramatic when it did on the next day.' The men in Will Bird's platoon relaxed and discussed what they would do in the future. Then the company sergeant major told Bird to get his section ready and into battle order – they were going to take Mons. The men protested, but the CSM simply said, 'Orders are orders.' Bird's men moved forward under German shrapnel and tear gas to relieve the Princess Pat's, firing at machine guns. A shell exploded, killing two of Bird's section. Bird knocked out the crew of a German machine gun with rifle grenades, and his war finally ended.

In 1911, a Prussian general had dismissed Canadians as 'trash, feeble adversaries.' At the beginning of the First World War, Canada had 3110 regular soldiers. By the end of it, 619,636 had served in the Canadian Army, and 59,544 of them had lost their lives. Canada's Hundred Days cost 45,830 casualties. As Lt. Gen. Sir Arthur Currie put it, the 'young whelps of the old lion' had regained the ground lost by the British in the first days of the war. The country's contribution to winning the First World War assured her of a separate place at the peace negotiations, despite British efforts to seat her with its delegation. The nation had come of age, at an enormous cost in blood and suffering.

Murdock MacPhee summarized the reasons for the success of the Canadian soldiers: 'We might have looked like a ragtag bunch, but we had real discipline. We'd heard in school all about the Thin Red Line, and wondered how well we'd do in battle. After we went into action we realized that we were better than we ever thought we were.'

Some of the troops on the Western Front marched to occupy Germany and others mustered at Kinmel Park, near Rhyl in North Wales, to await their return to Canada. A riot broke out over the slowness of the repatriation process during the bleak winter of 1918-19. Five soldiers died, and 23 were injured. Will Bird went on leave with his friend Tommy, and they had a fine time in London. Then Tommy felt feverish, and Bird took him to hospital. Two days later, his friend died of influenza, and 'the world crashed down around me.'

Meanwhile, some Canadians still served in a strange intervention in Russia. When Warrant Officer William Leask arrived in Vladivostok early in 1919 with the Canadian Expeditionary Force of about 2000 men, he saw Ross rifles stacked up like cord-wood on the docks, and seven-seater Studebaker cars with their tires rotted and tops torn to ribbons. These military supplies were part of the reason for the Canadian presence in Siberia. By the end of 1917, 648,000 tons of war goods choked up the port, and the Allies feared that they would fall into enemy hands when Russia left the war. Prime Minister Borden also believed that if a popular government arose in Siberia, the Canadians could trade with it. William Leask commanded a train taking ammunition up the Trans-Siberian Railway to Omsk, the headquarters of Admiral Kolchak, the leader of the White Russians fighting the Bolsheviks. The soldiers saw no action in Siberia, but the force lost 100 soldiers to Spanish flu in 1918 before leaving Canada, and 20 men through disease and accident in Russia. A detachment of Mounties, actor Raymond Massey, and a number of conscripts served with the CEF. Leask saw dead bodies lying for days in the open sewers in Vladivostok and was glad to leave the 'nasty, filthy, cold-blooded' country in the spring of 1919.

Some Canadians did get a chance to fight in Russia. In January 1918, 15 officers and 26 non-commissioned officers joined a 'hush-hush army' recruited in France. They ended up with Dunsterforce, an Allied army in northern Persia (now Iran). Here they tried to hold the Turks back from Baku, just over the border in Russia. On 31 August, Sgt. Ambrose Mahar, the only Canadian casualty, received a shoulder wound and as the Turks took Baku, Dunsterforce evacuated the city and then was

disbanded on 22 September 1918.

Canadian soldiers also went to Murmansk and Archangel in northern Russia to fight the 'Bolos' and protect the supplies delivered to those ports for the Tsarist forces. A Canadian battery, designated the 16th Brigade, Canadian Field Artillery, disembarked at Archangel as part of 'Operation Elope' on 3 October 1918, and fought well on the Dvina Front. The Canadians gave their British and American Allies lessons in fighting – and in looting, for which they had become famous on the Western Front. A battery of guns went into action on 11 November on the Dvina River. Bolsheviks attacked the gun pits from the rear, killing two Canadians, then Lt. Bradshaw turned the weapons around and drove back the enemy. At Spasskoe on 24 January 1919, a Canadian gun held off a 'Bolo' attack until shattered by enemy shot. So the intervenors retreated. The pattern of action on the Murmansk Front resembled that southeast of Archangel. 'Operation Syren' began in the summer of 1918 and involved short, sharp encounters with the Bolshevik troops. Major Peter Anderson had served in France, been captured, and escaped from a German prisoner of war camp. On 10 April, he took a mixed force in an armoured train from Segezha to Urosozero twenty miles away and smashed a Bolshevik offensive before it started. But during the summer of 1919, all Canadian soldiers left Russia.

And so ended Canada's participation in the First World War.

Above: *Canadian soldiers supervise Russian prisoners loading barges at Yemetskoe in May 1919, during the Allied intervention in Russia. Next to be loaded from the jetty are rolls of barbed wire – a feature of virtually every military operation of the war.*

Right: *The scene on Yonge Street during victory celebrations in Toronto on 11 November 1918. Similar scenes were witnessed in towns and cities throughout the country.*

In the Air

They are the knighthood of this war, without fear, without
reproach, and they recall the legendary days of chivalry,
not merely by the daring of their exploits, but by the
nobility of their spirit.

PRIME MINISTER LLOYD GEORGE, *Parliament* (1917)

Below: The aerodrome at the School of Gunnery, Beamsville, Ontario, in 1918.

As anonymous masses of men fought for small patches of shattered land on the Western Front, brightly-painted planes wheeled around in the sky above, attacking each other and falling in flames. The solitary exploits of air aces stood in contrast to life on the mass killing grounds and in the trenches.

The world's first air war attracted a particular type of Canadian, who transferred from the Canadian Expeditionary Force to the Royal Flying Corps. In all, about 20,000 Canadians served in the RFC or in the Royal Naval Air Service (RNAS), the air arm of the Royal Navy.

The first attempt to create a Canadian air force ended in a fiasco. On 16 September 1914, Sir Sam Hughes ordered the formation of the Canadian Aviation Corps. It acquired a commander, one other officer, and a Burgess-Dunne aeroplane, and went to Salisbury Plain with the CEF where it disintegrated in the damp and dismal winter of 1914-15. The plane fell apart, the commanding officer resigned his commission, and his companion, Lt. W. F. Sharpe, transferred to the RFC and died in an accident on 4 February 1915.

Canadians could only become fighter pilots by enlisting in another service, transferring to the RFC or the RNAS, or by sailing to Britain at their own expense and enlisting there. In the spring of 1915, however, the British began to recruit pilots in Canada who qualified at their own expense before being commissioned and sent to war. Thus most came from middle or upper class families. For $400, potential pilots received 500 minutes in the air at Canada's first flying school, set up on Toronto Island by J. A. D. McCurdy. On 11 July 1915, Homer Smith and Arthur Ince became the first two pilots to graduate from the school. On 14 December Ince shot down a German seaplane off the coast of Belgium – the first Canadian kill.

A Canadian recruiting advertisement, headed 'The All-Seeing Aviator,' began: 'The aeroplane upset many old ideas of Military Strategy. Surprise tactics of the enemy, once so effective, are now impossible as long as our aviators rule the air.' The RFC sought 'clear-headed, keen young men, 18 to 30 years of age' with 'fair education and sturdy physique.' The ad offered to send such people a booklet, 'Air Heroes in the Making.' A Royal Air Force flight surgeon, himself a pilot, stated that 'flying officers from overseas' – also known as 'colonials' and 'black troops' – had advantages over the British. He claimed that these men, accustomed to life in the open and to wearing little clothing, had not been coddled like the British!

Below: The aeroplane repair section, Camp Borden, Ontario, 1917. As many fliers died in accidents as in combat during World War I.

Right: *Lester Pearson, who became Prime Minister of Canada and winner of the Nobel Peace Prize, in the Royal Flying Corps.*

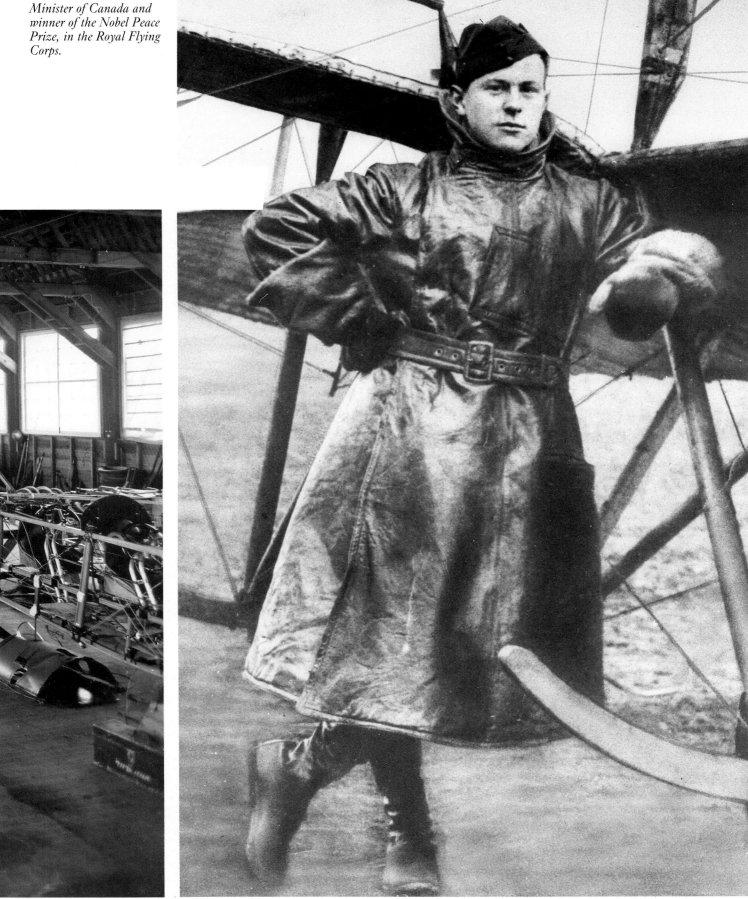

Canadians did, in fact, excel in aerial combat.

William Avery Bishop and Raymond Collishaw became the first and third top-scoring fighter pilots among the British fliers. 'Billy' Bishop shot down 72 enemy aircraft. A maverick and a loner, he fought authority as well as the enemy. Collishaw accounted for 60 enemy planes. His flair for personal leadership and teamwork inspired the pilots he led in the air above Europe and the members of the RAF squadron he commanded against the Bolsheviks in 1919-20.

Growing up in Owen Sound, the son of a county registrar, Billy Bishop learned to shoot squirrels with deadly accuracy. His school principal told Bishop's parents that 'the only thing your son is good at is fighting,' and at the Royal Military Academy he earned the reputation of being 'the worst cadet' the RMC ever had. Bishop joined a militia regiment when war broke out, and reached Britain in the summer of 1915. Mired in mud on the parade ground at Shorncliffe, an army camp he called 'military hell,' Bishop saw a fighter plane land nearby. The pilot had lost his way, and the Canadian decided that this was the only way to fight a war – 'up there above the

Left: *The legendary Billy Bishop, Canada's top-scoring war ace. Bishop remained in the air force after the war and rose to high rank.*

Above: *Billy Bishop and the Nieuport 17 Scout in which he attacked a German aerodrome and won the Victoria Cross.*

clouds and in the summer sunshine.' Transferring to the RFC, he gained his wings in 1916. A fellow flier described him as 'a fantastic shot but a terrible pilot.' After service in Britain, Bishop arrived in France in March 1917, and flew a Nieuport Scout with 60 Squadron. After shooting down his first plane on 25 March, Bishop narrowly escaped the fate of many pilots, more of whom died in accidents than in combat. A faulty engine forced him down among the British front line trenches.

On 31 March, Bishop filed a typical combat report: 'While on escort, I went to the assistance of another Nieuport being attacked by an Albatross Scout. I opened fire twice, the last time at 50 yards range, my tracers were seen to hit his machine in the center section. Albatross seemed to fall out of control, as he was in a spinning nose dive with his engine on. Albatross crashed at 7.30: Ref. 51B. 29-30.'
A pilot flying behind Bishop confirmed the kill, as

did members of an anti-aircraft battery.
Then came 'Bloody April.'
Major-General Sir Hugh Trenchard, commander of the RFC, insisted that his squadron commanders seek out and attack the enemy. He also established the policy of the 'full dinner table.' If a pilot went missing in combat in the morning, his replacement would be in place by the time the squadron sat down to dinner in the evening. In April 1917, the British had 365 fighters, and the Germans about 100. The Germans trained to fly in mutual support of each other, had superior fighters, and fought at the time and place of their own choosing. Between 4 and 8 April, the British lost 75 aircraft in combat, and another 56 in accidents. During that period, Billy Bishop shot down four enemy aircraft and two balloons. On 2 June 1917, Bishop took off alone, attacked a German aerodrome, shot down three Albatrosses and won the Victoria Cross.

After more victories, Bishop left France to be invested with the V.C., the Distinguished Service Order and the Military Cross at Buckingham Palace in August, and then returned to Canada. On 27 May 1918, Billy Bishop downed a German two-seater while in command of his squadron, the Flying Foxes, in France. Between that date and 19 June, the Canadian sent down another 25 German planes. Seeing his friends killed and wounded, Bishop developed a hatred of the Hun. But his attitude changed as his score rose. He shot down a two-seater, watching it disintegrate. The two men in it, like Allied pilots, did not wear parachutes and they fell screaming to the earth 4000 metres below.

Writing after the war, Bishop mentioned a 'feeling almost of friendship' on both sides among pilots who looked upon their work 'as a game and not as war.' Bishop tells of the 'Flying Pig,' a German observer-gunner so fat he could hardly fit into the cockpit. He fought bravely, despite being handicapped by a poor pilot, and Bishop's squadron treated him like a mascot, granting him immunity. But one day, a new British pilot failed to recognize the 'Flying Pig' and shot the German down. That night the squadron held a mess dinner to honour a brave enemy.

Raymond Collishaw, born in 1893 on Vancouver Island, joined the Canadian fisheries protection service after leaving school. Volunteering to fly when war broke out, he became a pilot with the Royal Naval Air Service. His first mission took him over Germany in a bomber in September 1916. He shot down his first plane on 15 February 1917 while flying a Sopwith Pup. Promoted in April, Collishaw led his all-Canadian 'Black Flight' against the Germans above the Ypres sector from May to July 1917. It became one of the most successful units on the Western Front, downing 67 planes, with Collishaw accounting for 32 of them.

In January 1918, Collishaw became commander of No. 3 (Naval) Squadron, and was not expected to fly in combat. But in June he took to the air, leading his men into battle on patrols three or four times a week. By the time he was relieved of command in October, Collishaw had recorded 60 victories.

In March 1919, Collishaw, now a lieutenant-colonel in the RAF, arrived in southern Russia in command of 47 Squadron, supporting White Russians under Baron Peter Wrangel against the Red Army. The unit's DH9 and 9A bombers and Sopwith Camel fighters, worn out and war-weary, soon developed problems. On the flight to the squadron's base at Beketovka, the engines of two Camels failed, a defective fuel pump crippled a third and the oil pressure pump of another fell off in flight.

The squadron gave a good account of itself under Collishaw's leadership, bombing Bolshevik headquarters at Tsaritsyn (now Volgograd) and shooting down enemy fighters: Collishaw accounted for three of them. But then the Reds surged forward, sending the White Russians fleeing. Collishaw supervised the withdrawal of 47 Squadron, which loaded its planes on a train and made a fighting retreat as the railway system in South Russia dissolved in chaos. Reaching Novorossiisk on the Black Sea, Collishaw's men watched as a tank was driven over their aged Camels – and some new DH9s still in their crates – to prevent them from falling into the hands of the Reds. They left the port on 27 March 1920. Collishaw survived the debacle – and a bout of typhus. Later he commanded squadrons in Iraq and Britain and took over the air force in Egypt in the Second World War. But Collishaw had no knack for office work. Moving to Fighter Command in 1941, he retired as an air vice-marshal in 1943, dying in West Vancouver on 29 September 1976.

Willy Barker won the Victoria Cross in October 1918. Like Bishop, he arrived in Britain with a mounted regiment, transferred to the RFC, served as an observer, took pilot training, then joined a fighter squadron. He shot down five enemy aircraft over France in October 1917, moving with his unit to Italy to prop up the crumbling front there. By the end of March 1918, Barker had accounted for ten enemy planes and nine observation balloons. In command of 66 Squadron, he shot down 16 enemy aircraft. Then he flew an Italian trimotor bomber to drop a secret agent behind enemy lines. Awarded two Medaglia d'Argento al Valor Militare by a grateful Italian government, Barker returned to England in September 1918 as an instructor.

Above: *Major Ray Collishaw, here seen in early 1918, downed 60 enemy planes.*

Right: *Major William George Barker won his Victoria Cross in October 1918, and died in a flying accident in 1930.*

Below: *Future Canadian pilots learn about the Curtiss JN-4 at No. 4 School of Aeronautics, University of Toronto, in 1917.*

Craving action, he returned to aerial combat for a short spell in France. On 27 October, flying alone in a Sopwith Snipe, Barker shot down an enemy two-seater. Then 60 German fighters jumped him. Wounded in the thigh, the Canadian fought back, downing three of them. Hit twice again, Barker crash-landed his plane, and barely recovered from his wounds and injuries. This final encounter with the enemy won the pilot the V.C.

About half of the Canadians who flew overseas during the First World War came from urban areas, and a third of them hailed from Toronto. A high proportion of all pilots had been white collar workers or students. The wartime careers of two of them show how sharply their destinies differed, and reveal the dulling monotony of war in the air.

John Bernard ('Don') Brophy, born in Ottawa in 1893 to an engineer, loved sports and athletics, and flunked his first year at McGill University. The outbreak of the war gave focus to his life, and at first he treated it like another sport. Learning to fly at Toronto Island, Brophy left Ottawa as a second lieutenant in the RFC on 8 December 1915, for further training in England. By the time he arrived in France

in May 1916, the nature of war in the air had changed. At first pilots had dropped bombs, carried observers, directed artillery shoots, and done a wide range of duties. The planes and pilots had limited capabilities for killing.

By the fall of 1915, the first true fighter planes, called 'scouts,' appeared. The Fokker EI had a machine gun fixed to fire through its rotating propeller. These planes swept the skies until the British introduced the slightly faster De Havilland 2, which mounted a fixed machine gun. Posted to 21 Squadron, Brophy flew an outdated, unstable RE7 in the dangerous skies above the battlefront. An observer sat in front of the pilot; Brophy referred to him as a 'shock absorber.' Armed with a Lewis light machine gun on a flexible mounting, the observer had to ensure that he did not hit the propeller or shred the wings on either side of the cockpit when firing.

By 1916, the average life expectancy of a British pilot was three weeks. Brophy lasted five months. From his diary he emerges as a bumptious yet brave and stoical young man. While learning to fly in England, Brophy pondered on the possibility of being 'reduced to hash by a collision with the earth.' On 23 March 1916, while flying at 1400 metres, 14 kilometres from base, the engine of Brophy's plane quit. Later he wrote in his diary that, 'This annoyed me to a certain extent and I decided to fly no further. . . . ' Two weeks later, the engine of his plane failed again. Brophy landed, pumped petrol into it, and monkeyed with the engine before being able to take off again. Four days later, the engine of the plane he was flying quit yet again, but this time Brophy managed to stay in the air.

On 26 May 1916, Brophy flew across the enemy lines in France for the first time, patrolling from Souchez to Arras and Sommecourt. Setting out early in the morning two days later, the engine of his plane cut out, a wing tip hit the ground, and the nose followed. The undercarriage and propeller flew off, and the plane spun around. Brophy wrote: 'The engine proceeded to run very well without the prop on, so I switched off and got out.' Walking back to the aerodrome, he sought another plane. He tried to start the only serviceable one for an hour and a half, failed to do so, and gave up. Through Brophy's diary runs the new language of the fighter pilots. Flying 'buses,' accompanied by other 'garçons,' Brophy watched anti-aircraft guns throw 'archie' at him. Between these times of terror came 'dud days,' when weather grounded the primitive planes.

On 1 July 1916, as the British advanced on the first day of the Battle of the Somme, Brophy bombed the railway and stores at Bapaume. When he landed, the pilot found a shrapnel bullet lodged in the wood of his plane. On the following day, Brophy bombed a chateau housing a German headquarters, but could not see any damage from the 150-kilo bomb he had dropped. In fact, these bombs buried themselves in the ground and did no damage if dropped from heights over 1500 metres.

By his fourth month in France, Brophy's squadron had no planes to fly. But on 4 September, flying

again, Brophy, with yet another plane whose engine was 'going badly,' saw below him the area over which the British had advanced on the Somme – 'a huge brown patch, with a few thousand shell holes to the square mile.' As the Canadian pilot continued to patrol, he saw his friends die around him. Don Brophy won no medals, receiving a Mention in Dispatches for destroying an enemy plane. After a spell of leave in November, Brophy chased Zeppelins over Britain, almost catching one of these huge airships which the Germans used to bomb Britain.

At 3:55 on the afternoon of Christmas Eve, 1916, Brophy climbed into a BE12 single-seater fighter and headed for the open sky. There he dived sharply, then looped the loop perfectly. As he turned to land, the plane spiralled down and hit the ground, nose first, at 250 kilometres an hour. Strained beyond its limits, part of the plane had come apart, and Don Brophy met the death about which he had mused while training to fly in combat.

By the time Harold Warnica Price, a dentist's son from Toronto, entered the RFC just before his twentieth birthday in late 1916, pilot training had been formalized and professionalized. Price reached Britain in November 1916. An introspective, puri-

Above: *Canadian airmen learn how to swing a propeller at Camp Borden, Ontario, in 1917.*

tanical youth brought up in a strict Methodist household, he loved to fly. When the engine of his Farman 'Shorthorn' stopped on a training flight, Price compared the feeling of falling to the 'exhilaration of a steep toboggan slide.' He won his wings on 25 May 1917, and looked forward to going to France. Posted to 63 Squadron of the RFC, he went instead to Mesopotamia (now Iraq), the land between the Tigris and Euphrates. Here he contended with heat, humidity, dust and disease while fighting a handful of German pilots flying for the Turks. He also bombed troops, aerodromes, and supply dumps in the empty desert between Baghdad and Samarra. Only six officers and 70 other ranks remained on duty after the squadron's arrival in Mesopotamia. Sandfly fever, heatstroke and other ailments had felled the other 24 officers and 130 airmen. A storm in April 1918 did more damage to their planes and their base in two hours than the enemy inflicted in three years.

Price's diary tells of headaches, fevers, and stomach problems, as well as about defective engines. He described one as sounding 'like a biscuit tin full of empty shell cases.' If the pilots crash-landed in the desert, an official document said they should treat being robbed by Bedouin tribesmen as a joke. If the locals turned nasty, they had the choice of 'hanging on until possible British assistance arrives, or of selling lives dearly.'

On 1 April 1918, the RFC and the RNAS became a new, independent service – the Royal Air Force. Price makes no mention of the event in his diary. At the end of that month, flying from Baghdad, he bombed and machine-gunned columns of Turkish infantry and cavalry. On other missions he saw troops waiting to surrender to the British, but did not have the heart to strafe them. On 8 June, Price had 'a pretty good crash.' Both he and the observer emerged unscathed, but the 'bus' looked 'a most unholy mess.'

The monotony of life in Mesopotamia was relieved when Price met what he called 'genuine Canadians,' including Reg Roome, an artillery officer from Halifax. Bored with training after going overseas with the Canadian Second Division, Roome went absent without leave from his unit in search of a commission in the Royal Field Artillery. The British recognized his initiative, and by Sep-

Below: *Learning to fire a machine gun in a JN-4 at the School of Aerial Gunnery, Camp Borden, 1917.*

tember 1915 Roome was with a battery in the Ypres Salient. Every one of its officers was killed or wounded, and Roome recalled calmly that he 'knew it was only a matter of time before I was hit.' Wounded after 18 months in battle, he recovered and then discovered that he had been posted to Mesopotamia. Bent on returning to his unit, he went to the War Office, only to be advised by a colonel, 'Don't be a bloody fool. You've done your time in Europe. Go and fight the Turks.'

But Roome found the war in Mesopotamia 'no mean show' and his experiences, like those of the soldiers on the Western Front, stood in marked contrast to those of the airmen. The airmen flew short but dangerous missions and returned to their bases, beds and messes. Roome's battery covered 50 miles in four days on half-rations and then went into battle. His war ended when the Turks signed an armistice on 30 October 1918.

Price's war went on. The collapse of Turkish power and the Russian Revolution created a power vacuum in the Middle East and the Arabs rose, seeking independence. Price flew missions against them. In his free time he shot game. On 7 March 1919, he went into hospital with a severe fever. Eight Canadians served with 63 Squadron, and one died in action. But of all the 101 officers who served with the unit in Mesopotamia, only six died in combat or in accidents.

Price had entertained the idea of becoming a doctor, setting up a practice in Mecca, and leading a Christian revival there. He did obtain a medical degree, but moved to Calgary and died there on 10 June 1975.

Canada created its own air force just as the war ended. In December 1916, the British authorized the formation of the Royal Flying Corps, Canada, and the establishment of training squadrons in Canada. Pilot training, with heavy emphasis on gunnery, began at Camp Borden, Ontario, in the first week of May 1917, and the country's first military airport was completed at the same location on 2 June. The United States had entered the war in April, and Americans came to Borden to train. Over the following winter Canadians travelled to Fort Worth, Texas, to instruct American pilots. In 1918, a gunnery school built at Beamsville, Ontario, taught the newest techniques in aerial combat.

The establishment of the RAF forced Canada to create its own air arm. In November 1918, two all-Canadian units came together at Upper Heyford, Oxfordshire, to form Squadrons 1 and 2 of the Canadian Air Force. Too late to see combat, the squadrons disbanded in 1920. The Canadian government set up an Air Board in Ottawa and trained pilots and ground crew for a 'non-permanent' air arm. The Royal Canadian Air Force formally came into being on 1 April 1924. Willy

Below: No. 1 Squadron of the newly formed Royal Canadian Air Force, seen here at Upper Heyford in England, came into being in November 1918, too late to see combat. The planes are Sopwith Dolphins.

Barker served briefly as its first director before being fatally injured in a plane crash at Rockcliffe Air Station, Ottawa, and dying on 12 March 1930.

The Victoria Cross winner had gone into business with Billy Bishop, running a commercial aviation company that carried passengers and goods. The two aces stunted above the Canadian National Exhibition in 1920, terrifying people and losing their contract. So the partners liquidated the unprofitable venture.

Billy Bishop, made an honorary air vice-marshal in the RCAF in 1935, helped to develop the British Commonwealth Air Training Plan which graduated 131,553 pilots, navigators, bomb aimers, wireless operators, air gunners and flight engineers between 1940 and 1945. Bishop presided over many of the parades where pilots received their wings. They had 150 hours of training, compared to the 18 and a half that Bishop received before he put up his wings. Billy Bishop died in bed on 11 September 1956, just before the chill dawn, the time at which he had set out on so many patrols. The ace had shown what Napoleon called the rarest kind of courage – 'the courage of early morning.' But as Bishop set out at dawn, he silently prayed: 'God give me strength. God be with me now.'

During the 1970s, Canadians rediscovered the country's leading air ace of the First World War. John Gray's two-man play, *Billy Bishop Goes to War* (1978), caught the pilot's wild daring and sense of humour. The well-known Canadian tendency to disparage heroes emerged in *The Kid Who Couldn't Miss*, a National Film Board production on the life of Billy Bishop, made in 1982. It cast doubts on the feat that won the ace the Victoria Cross, and roused the fury of many ex-servicemen. The Senate held an enquiry into the making of the film, which went out with a statement that it combined elements of both reality and fiction.

To the war-weary world of 1917, Billy Bishop represented the ideal warrior – not a mud-stained wretch huddling in fear as the German guns shredded his comrades, but a knightly figure combining chivalry and schoolboy daring. The Germans called him 'Hell's Handmaiden,' and Bishop admitted to strafing downed airmen and killing the crew of a two-seater when the observer's gun jammed. Toward the end of his life he admitted that the public loved the 'red hot, hurray-for-our-side stuff' in his 1917 book *Winged Warfare*. But now he found the book so terrible he could not read it – 'It turns my stomach.'

But for every ace who found fame and glory in the skies of the First World War, there were a dozen Don Brophys, decent young men who also had the courage of early morning but lacked Bishop's luck and skill and died through accidents or plummeting to the ground in their flaming aircraft.

AT SEA

Canada's . . . naval contribution to the World War was so
small . . . that no Canadian naval history need be recorded
here.
The Cambridge History of the British Empire (1930)

Canada built its first 'warship' to protect its resources, not the land and the people. The *Canada*, commissioned in 1904, carried two 12-pounder guns and a crew of 50 to guard the East Coast fisheries.

In 1897, Prime Minister Wilfrid Laurier had been pressured to provide Canadian dollars to build British dreadnoughts. But Canadians wanted their own navy, and on 4 May 1910, Parliament passed the Naval Services Act and Rear-Admiral Charles Kingsmall, born in Guelph, Ontario, took command of it. The British sold Canada two elderly cruisers, *Niobe* and *Rainbow*, one for each coast. Crews trained on the job and many deserted because of the penny-pinching attitude the government took toward its new navy.

As war appeared inevitable, Richard McBride, premier of British Columbia, became alarmed at the possibility of the German cruiser *Leipzig*, operating in the Pacific, attacking his province's coasts and shipping. So he bought two submarines from a Seattle company. Destined for Chile, they were instead sailed north by an American crew. Two Canadian naval officers boarded the submarines on the night of 4 August 1914, paying for the vessels with a cheque for $1.15 million. In the same month, Jack Ross, a wealthy naval reserve officer, bought the fast steam yacht *Tarantula* from William K. Vanderbilt, fitted her out at his own expense and sold it to the Canadian government for a dollar. The yacht became HMCS *Tuna*. In the spring of 1915, Ross bought the yacht *Winchester*. Refitted and armed with two 12-pounder guns and a torpedo tube, she became HMCS *Grilse*.

When war broke out, *Rainbow* set out to sea from Esquimault half-manned with a green crew and lacking proper ammunition. *Niobe*, stationed in Halifax, patrolled the sealanes between that city and New York, but kept breaking down and ended her career as a depot ship. *Grilse* sailed from Halifax to Bermuda in December 1916, and almost sank on the way. She spent the war patrolling the Atlantic approaches to Canada, as did HMCS *Canada*. The two Canadian submarines, C1 and C2, moved from British Columbia to Halifax, but kept breaking down and never became operational.

In 1918, Canada's navy tried to protect shipping off the East Coast from attacks by three large German submarines which had greater firepower than most of the Canadian ships. The U-boats sank a number of schooners and small steamers without interference from Canada's navy. The captain of HMCS *Hochelaga*, an armed yacht, turned away on sighting U-156 off Newfoundland on 25 August, and was later dismissed from the service.

At the end of the war, Canada's navy had 100 vessels and 5500 members. About 3000 sailors recruited for the Royal Canadian Navy served with the Royal Navy, and many joined the RN directly. The first Canadians to die in battle, four young midshipmen, went down with HMS *Good Hope* during the Battle of Coronel off the coast of Chile on 1 November 1914. Canadian sailors showed great gallantry when war came to Halifax on 6 December 1917. Just before nine o'clock on the morning of that day, the French ship *Mont Blanc*, laden with explosives, made her way toward Bedford Basin to join a convoy. Sailing out of Bedford Basin came the *Imo*, a Belgian relief ship. At the Narrows, which join the basin to Halifax harbor, the two vessels collided. As steel grated on steel, a shower of sparks ignited the deckload of benzine on the *Mont Blanc*. Her crew abandoned ship, pulling frantically for the Dartmouth shore. Watchers crowded the Halifax waterfront as the burning ship headed toward the Richmond piers in the north end of the city.

Sailors from *Niobe*'s steam pinnace boarded the *Mont Blanc* to secure a hawser and tow the burning ship away from land. Then the French vessel exploded as fire turned her 2600 tons of picric acid, gun cotton and TNT into a ball of intensely hot gas. Two thousand people died, most of them in the working class and factory area of north end Halifax. *Niobe* lay 700 metres from the explosion. The blast blew down one of her funnels and the tidal wave that followed tore the old cruiser from her moorings. In the old naval hospital, now housing the Royal Naval College of Canada, cadets watching the burning ship reeled back from the windows, blinded by flying glass, as the *Mont Blanc* exploded.

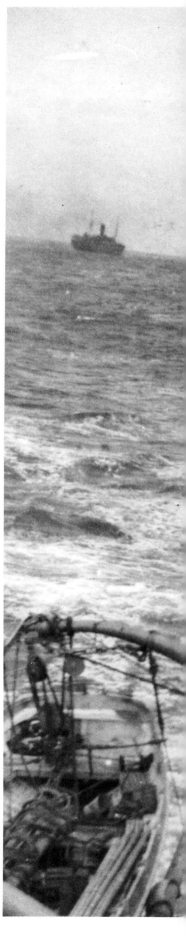

Right: *The convoy carrying the Canadian Expeditionary Force in the North Atlantic, en route to Britain, 8 October 1914.*

Left: *The yacht* Waturus *before it became HMCS* Hochelaga *in the Royal Canadian Navy between 1915 and 1920.*

Below: *The devastation in the North End of Halifax after the* Mont Blanc *and the* Imo *collided on 6 December 1917. The* Imo *lies shattered on the Dartmouth shore.*

John Gammon served as master-at-arms on *Niobe*. On the morning of 6 December he was supervising divers building a concrete foundation for a wharf crane. The explosion of the *Mont Blanc* blew him onto his stomach, and he first thought that a German submarine had crept into the harbour to shell the dockyard. Recovering quickly, Gammon rescued the two divers, then went in search of his family. One daughter and his badly-injured wife survived the explosion. But of their other two children, Gammon never found any trace.

A ship approaching Halifax harbour saw an umbrella-shaped cloud rise 4000 metres above the city, as the *Mont Blanc* vanished in the greatest man-made explosion until the atom bomb was dropped on Hiroshima on 6 August 1945.

The munitions on the *Mont Blanc*, destined for the Western Front, killed and mutilated thousands of Canadians. The fate of John Gammon's family served as a harbinger of future wars in which civilians as well as soldiers would be on the front lines. The First World War had been fought on land, at sea and in the air in scattered localities.

The next war would be truly world-wide.

And some idealistic, adventurous and footloose Canadians had a taste of this new kind of war when they served in the prelude to it – the Spanish Civil War of 1936-39.

The
Spanish
Civil War

> . . . going to fight there was one of the few things I am
> proud of having done. It is always better to fight for what
> you believe in.
> HUGH GARNER, *One Damn Thing After Another!* (1973)

Hugh Garner arrived in Spain in March 1937 to fight in the Civil War wearing a brand new suit, a homburg hat and spats. He had been working in a clothing store when he decided to fight against fascism. Like the other volunteers he carried in his suitcase a First World War American army uniform, a khaki sheepskin coat, a first-aid kit, socks and underwear bought at an army surplus store in New York City.

Garner grew up poor in Toronto's Cabbagetown, and drifted around North America during the 1930s. He describes his fellow volunteers as 'communist fanatics, idealists and adventurers.' Few had military training, but they went bravely into battle with obsolete arms against the professional armies of General Franco. He led the Spanish generals who revolted on 17-18 July 1936, fearing a Communist takeover of their country after a left-wing government came to power in February. Hitler and Mussolini provided arms and troops to the 'Nationalists,' and the Soviet Union contributed equipment and advisors to the 'Republicans' and organized an international brigade to fight with them. Britain, France and the other western democracies remained neutral, as did Canada.

The Mackenzie-Papineau battalion of the International Brigade – the 'Mac-Paps' – came into being on 1 July 1937 through what its historian calls a 'combination of circumstances, initiative and luck.' Americans outnumbered Canadians three to one and provided most of the officers. The battalion distinguished itself at Fuentes de Ebro in October 1937, charging across a bullet-swept plain. William Kardash of Winnipeg led an attack with five tanks. He was the only survivor when his tank was set on fire. The Mac-Paps went into battle again at Teruel in January 1938. Moorish cavalry waving banners charged its command post. Edward C. Smith, a former journalist described as looking like 'a beefy college professor,' rallied his men and cut down the charging Moors with machine guns.

In the spring of 1938, the Mac-Paps joined the straggle of soldiers retreating beyond the Ebro River in northern Spain. Near Gandesa, they stopped an attack by Nationalist tanks in April, but when the battalion left the war in September, it had only 38 effective members.

Hugh Garner's high idealism did not survive long in that savage war. He served with the 17th (Abraham Lincoln) Battalion of the 15th International Brigade which had lost half its numbers at the Battle of Jarama on 27 February 1937, just before he joined it. The dead included a young man from Cabbagetown, an amateur wrestler with whom Garner had gone to school. On 5 July Garner, a member of the battalion's heavy machine gun section, moved into

the Battle of Brunete. With the gun out of action, Garner spent the day as an infantryman, pressed into the wheat stubble, watching his comrades cut down like weeds as they advanced across open ground without artillery support. Fear tasted like a copper coin in his mouth.

Garner survived the battle, but he annoyed an officer who had sent him and the other three members of the machine gun section to dig trenches a mere 100 metres from the enemy lines by sneaking away to Madrid, where he joined the Anarchists on the El Pardo Front. Missing his comrades and his mail, Garner rejoined the International Brigade, narrowly escaping execution as a deserter. The volunteers found themselves used as cannon fodder in suicidal attacks on enemy positions, and referred to the fanatical Communists who directed their actions as 'Red Rotarians' and 'Comicals.'

Above: *A plane of the German Condor Legion bombs Valencia in 1939.*

Top right: *General Francisco Franco, the fascist dictator, whose invasion of Spain in 1936 touched off the civil war.*

Right: *The Alcazar in Toledo under attack by the Republicans in 1936. Franco relieved the fortress in September.*

Above: *British members of the International Brigade march through a village in France after leaving Spain in 1938.*

Left: *Republican soldiers move into action in a town in Catalonia.*

Top: *Nationalist guards on patrol in a disputed quarter of Barcelona.*

Right: *Burned-out cars in Barcelona, a centre of Republican resistance.*

Emerging from the gloom of the cathedral in Alcalá de Henares into bright morning sunshine, Garner noticed a small truck marked 'Canadian Blood Transfusion Service.' Nearby stood a slight man with 'Canada' flashes on his coveralls, and the future writer was introduced to Dr. Norman Bethune, who would become a Chinese hero and a Canadian legend after his death.

Born in 1890, the son of a Presbyterian minister in Gravenhurst, Ontario, Bethune served as a stretcher bearer in France in 1915, was wounded and returned to Canada to complete his medical degree. His classmates described Bethune as 'a distinct individualist' and 'a bit odd, a bit peculiar.' In university he expressed interest in socialism and the needs of ordinary people. After contracting pulmonary tuberculosis, Bethune developed new ways of treating the disease. He joined the Communist Party in 1935 after a visit to the Soviet Union. The Spanish Civil War provided Bethune with a cause, and an outlet for his energy and innovative abilities. He told a friend that democracy would either die or survive in Spain. Arriving in besieged Madrid on 3 November 1936, Bethune found a need – a blood transfusion service at the front. He seemed to love the smell of danger, taking his truck close to the fighting, providing up to 100 transfusions to the wounded in one day, and seeing the colour return to their faces as they received the blood. But Bethune soon fell afoul of the Communists controlling the Republican Army, who claimed that he was not disciplined. Tired and frustrated, Bethune left Spain in May 1937 to raise funds for the Republicans in Canada.

In July 1937, a minor clash between Chinese and Japanese troops turned into a major war. Bethune saw the battle there as part of the same conflict between democracy and despotism that was being played out in Spain. He went to join the 8th Route Army, led by Mao Zedong and Chou En Lai, in the Shanxi-Hobei region. Bethune devoted himself completely to serving the soldiers of the Red Army, using his own blood for transfusions, teaching, innovating, writing textbooks, reorganizing medical services, and establishing a model hospital, which was destroyed by the Japanese just after it was completed. One biography of Bethune has Chinese guerrillas charging into battle, shouting, 'Attack! Bethune is with us.'

While operating on a soldier with a broken leg on 28 October 1939, Bethune cut the middle finger of his left hand. A few days later he put his bare hand into a wound in the head of a soldier and the cut became infected. Pai Chu En, as the Chinese called him, died of blood poisoning on 12 November at Huang Shiko in northern China. As he lay dying, Bethune wrote that the last two years had been 'the most significant, the most meaningful' of his life. He had been lonely, but had found his highest fulfillment among his 'beloved comrades.'

Jean Ewen also served with the 8th Route Army as a nurse, working with Norman Bethune. Mao eulogized the Canadian doctor in an essay after his death, but Ewen's account of the man shows just how vulnerable and human the hero was. She presents him as an irascible, impatient man, unable to accept himself and his own limitations, who treated her like a servant, insisting that she never call him by his first name. After they parted company, Bethune wrote to her saying he felt she was too young for the work she was doing, and did not appreciate the seriousness of the cause she served.

But Jean Ewen catches the essence of the man when she tells of seeing him share his food with abandoned children, instilling confidence in frightened patients, and exercising his remarkable gifts as a surgeon and healer.

Although Ewen's father was a Communist, she did not go to China for the cause. Graduating as a nurse in 1933 when jobs were scarce, the young woman from Saskatchewan accepted an offer to work with the Franciscans in central China. She spent four years in the country, becoming fluent in the language, and obviously came to like the people. When the Communist Party of Canada sent out an appeal for nurses to serve with the 8th Route Army, Jean Ewen answered it and found that one of her jobs would be to look after Dr. Bethune. They travelled to China together early in 1938. Ewen delivered babies and attended emaciated, pain-stricken soldiers in dirty, blood-stained uniforms, staying just ahead of the advancing Japanese. She asked a Chinese doctor for anti-tetanus shots for a man with lockjaw. He just laughed at her innocence, and the man died 12 hours later. Ewen met Chou En Lai, who believed Canada to be a wild country inhabited by Indians, a few Frenchmen and the

Left: *Dr. Norman Bethune, Canadian surgeon and hero to the Chinese, in Madrid, February 1937.*

Dionne quintuplets. Escaping from the dying city of Hankow on an overloaded boat, Ewen lost her purse, camera and film – and almost her life – when Japanese planes blew it up and strafed the passengers. She saw a peasant woman cradling the body of her dead two-year-old daughter in her arms, wailing, 'wake up.' Reaching safety in Shanghai, Ewen volunteered to return to work in the base hospital of the Fourth Army. On 5 March 1939, Japanese planes flattened it. Time stood still during the raid, Ewen recalls, and when it ended she went back to caring for the wounded. This Canadian nurse, an unknown heroine, left Shanghai on the last boat out as war erupted in Europe.

Hugh Garner, working for three dollars a day in the tobacco fields of southern Ontario, heard of Canada's declaration of war over the radio. He returned to Toronto, and joined the 23rd Medium Battery, Royal Canadian Artillery. Left behind as a suspected Communist when the battery went overseas, Garner offered a colonel two choices – discharge him, or he would desert. Let out of the army, Garner hitchhiked to Halifax and joined the navy. He served in eight small ships between June 1940 and October 1945, rising from rating to chief petty officer. In his novel, *Storm Below*, Garner tells of the war at sea from the point of view of the men in the mess deck who served on the wild, heaving North Atlantic.

Only in the 1970s did Canadians come to appreciate the deeds of those who served in the International Brigade, and the National Film Board made a documentary about them. One estimate puts the number of Canadians on the Republican side in the Spanish Civil War at 1239, and 385 of these are known to have died in action.

Below: *Shanghai under Japanese air attack in 1937.*

The
Second
World War

ON LAND

Now therefore We do hereby Declare and Proclaim that a
State of War with the German Reich exists and has
existed in our Dominion of Canada as and from the tenth
day of September 1939
CANADA GAZETTE, 10 September 1939

On the evening of 9 September 1939, all of Canada's Members of Parliament save one voted to follow Britain and declare war on Germany. The official announcement of this in the *Canada Gazette* on the following day, however, appeared under the name of King George VI.

Across Canada unemployed men sought recruiting offices to serve a country that had ignored their abilities in peacetime. In September 1939, unemployment stood at 306,000 in Canada, and during that month 54,884 men enlisted.

The government had starved the armed forces of resources in the years between the wars. The regular army numbered about 4000, and its main role had been to train the Permanent Active Militia, which also had about 4000 members. Expenditure on the militia came to about $900 per man-year in the 1920s. Harry Foster joined Strathcona's Horse in 1924 after graduating from the Royal Military College. By 1929 he was a brevet-captain – he had the rank, but not the pay. When his fiancée's father opposed their marriage, he claimed that he 'couldn't afford the price of an elopement ladder' on his pay. In 1930, Foster went to Saskatchewan for cavalry training; the horse remained the main motive force in the army at that time. In 1933 the Princess Patricia's received a wire from National Defence Headquarters telling them to lay off 20 men because they lacked the money to pay them. The regiment also had to borrow paint from the navy when Ottawa refused to provide $20 for barrack room renovations.

Even in 1937, the army had no tanks. It received two in 1938 from Britain, and another 14 light tanks arrived just before war broke out. In 1938-39, the country spent $34.8 million on her armed forces, with about half of this going to the militia. A 1937 photo shows air raid practice, with the soldiers wearing swords and firing rifles into the air.

An advanced party from Canada arrived in London in November 1939 to establish Canadian Military Headquarters near Canada House. On 16 December, the ships carrying the first contingent of the 1st Canadian Division sailed up the Clyde. The troops moved to barracks in Aldershot in time to experience the coldest January since 1894. Here they trained and waited to go into battle.

On 18 April, a 1300-strong Canadian assault force set out to attack Trondheim Fiord after the Germans invaded Norway. But it turned back because of the strength of enemy forces there.

Above: *The eager Canadian beaver joins the British lion on this propaganda poster issued by the Director of Public Information.*

Right: *The National Film Board, created in May 1939, encouraged Canadians to fight the overseas enemy – not each other – during the war.*

Page 96: *Artist R. Filipowski combined the Vimy Monument and the words of John McCrea's famous poem to inspire Canadians.*

THE TORCH; BE YOURS TO HOLD IT HIGH!
IF YE BREAK FAITH WITH US WHO DIE
WE SHALL NOT SLEEP, THOUGH POPPIES GROW
IN FLANDERS FIELDS.

McCREA.

ISSUED BY THE DIRECTOR OF PUBLIC INFORMATION, OTTAWA, UNDER THE AUTHORITY OF HON. J. T. THORSON, MINISTER OF NATIONAL WAR SERVICES.

On 10 May 1940, the Germans unleashed their *blitzkrieg*. In this lightning war, their armoured panzers rolled through Holland and Belgium, cutting the British and French armies in half. Five days later the Dutch Army surrendered, and as Belgium collapsed the commander of the British Expeditionary Force, Lord Gort, ordered an evacuation through Dunkirk. He asked for Canadian troops to hold a bridgehead there, but they stayed in Britain to repel an expected German invasion. Lt. Gen. 'Andy' McNaughton, the Canadian commander, insisted that his troops fight together and not be split into 'penny packets' and fed into places where the British generals saw a need for them.

On 12 June, eight days after the last soldier left the beaches of Dunkirk, the 1st Canadian Infantry Brigade landed at Brest. Two days later the Germans entered Paris, the French army disintegrated, and the Canadian troops did an about-turn and headed back whence they came. By the time the recall order reached them, brigade headquarters and the 48th Highlanders of Canada had reached Sable-sur-Sarthe, about 250 kilometres southwest of Paris. With troops on the engine, two men with Tommy guns on the tender, and weapons bristling from every window, the train headed back to Brest. Luck favoured them. At Rennes a switching error sent them to St. Malo, where they found a British ship that took them to Southampton on 16 June. The troops at Brest had to leave behind all their vehicles

and equipment. Instead of destroying his guns as ordered, Lt. Col. Roberts of the 1st Field Regiment put them on board, and also saved some British anti-aircraft guns.

The Canadian Army lost six men in France. One died in a motorcycle accident and five were captured, although four of them later escaped.

Back in Britain, the Canadian troops awaited the German invasion during the 'sitzkrieg.' So short of weapons were the beleaguered British that Canada shipped over 75,000 Ross rifles for issue to the Home Guard.

Canadians garrisoned Iceland in June 1940, after the Germans took over Denmark. In August 1941, troops took part in a raid on Spitzbergen, removing Russian miners, blowing up machinery, and setting fire to coal stocks and fuel oil on the Norwegian-owned island. Tunnelers from Canada dug chambers in the Rock of Gibraltar, and the Van Doos guarded Buckingham Palace. On 5 November 1941, the first members of the Canadian Women's Army Corps arrived in Britain. On Christmas Day, 1941, members of a Canadian army unit fought the Black Watch in the streets of Camberley using boots and broken bottles. The battle ended when the Scots drew bayonets and chased the Canadians out of town. Reports circulated of drunken Canadian soldiers 'yelling like redskins,' grabbing women in the tranquil streets of Oxford.

Bored, homesick, on poor rations in a country

Previous page: *Jack Bernard's five-year-old son Warren reaches for his father's hand as a Canadian contingent leaves for Europe in 1940.*

Above: *Canadian soldiers of the Second Division and members of the Royal Canadian Air Force bid farewell to Canada as their ship leaves Halifax in June 1940.*

Top right: *A French Canadian soldier holds his daughter as a train takes them to an East Coast port where he will embark for Britain, November 1940.*

Right: *Prime Minister Winston Churchill greets Prime Minister Mackenzie King in London in September 1941.*

with a habit of rendering even good food inedible, Canadian soldiers often found the people of the island reserved and unfriendly. Some units took the initiative in holding children's parties, helping farmers, and engaging in rescue work. Gunner Jack Chambers of the Royal Canadian Horse Artillery won the George Medal for rescuing a firemen during a London blitz. When German bombers hit Liverpool in a week of attacks in May 1941, Capt. D. C. Heggie, a medical officer, looked after air raid victims trapped in ruined buildings, winning the George Medal. In Scotland, the Canadian Forestry Corps cut down trees the way they did at home – at chest height.

Prime Minister Mackenzie King came to England in late August 1941, and at a luncheon in his honor Winston Churchill touched upon the state of the 'gallant Canadian Corps.' He 'felt very much for them' because they had not yet had 'a chance of coming to close quarters with the enemy.' Had the Germans invaded, he went on, the Canadians would have been 'the first to be hurled into a counterstroke' against them.

Churchill's words foreshadowed the role that Canadian troops would be called upon to play, again and again, in the Second World War. In their first encounter with Germans, and their single battle with the Japanese Army, they showed courage and tenacity in attacking Dieppe and defending Hong Kong. And at both places, they died in the hundreds.

Hong Kong

The minute I got off the boat in Hong Kong, I realized
that if the Japanese attacked, they'd wipe us out.
PRIVATE WILF LYNCH, IN TED FERGUSON'S *Desperate Siege*
(1980)

The first Canadian troops to see action in the Second World War engaged Japanese infantry in the New Territories of Hong Kong on 11 December 1941. D Company of the Winnipeg Grenadiers formed part of 'C Force' sent to garrison this remote outpost of empire at the request of the British government. Together with a battalion from the Royal Rifles of Canada, the Canadian troops had left Vancouver on 27 October 1941, under the command of Brigadier J. K. Lawson.

When the Japanese declared war on the United States and Britain in December through their attack on Pearl Harbor, Hong Kong became one of their first conquests. The colony could neither be held nor relieved, and a quarter of the 1975 members of 'C Force' died in battle or while prisoners of the Japanese. War came to Hong Kong on the morning of 8 December. The Japanese easily broke the colony's defence system, the Gin Drinkers' Line,

Right: *The Canadian Pacific takes troops to Vancouver to embark for the futile attempt to defend Hong Kong, November 1941.*

Below: *The Japanese conquest of Hong Kong, completed on Christmas Day, 1941.*

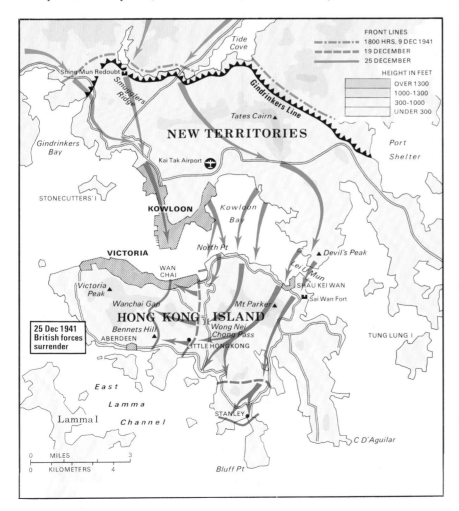

two days later. The British, Canadian and Indian troops retreated to positions on the island of Hong Kong. The Grenadiers formed part of the West Brigade, and the Royal Rifles joined the East Brigade. Brigadier Lawson set up his command post in the Wong Nei Chong Gap, between the two groups, on the road that cut through the center of the island. The troops fought from strongpoints, and the

Canadians formed part of a mobile flying column sent to deal with Japanese attacks. Backed by artillery and air power, the Japanese landed on the island on the evening of 18 December. Infiltrators seized Fort Sai Wan and killed the defenders. When Major Bishop of the Rifles requested artillery fire on the fort, he was told that it was still held by friendly troops. Bishop went to investigate the situation and

Left: *A bullet-scarred house on the ridge, between Wong Nei Gap and Repulse Bay, where Canadian troops fought and died in hopeless battle against the Japanese.*

Below: *The Repulse Bay Hotel, once an earthly paradise, became the site of a last stand by the defenders of the doomed colony.*

NEAR THIS SITE
WERE EXECUTED
H6016. SGT. J. O. PAYNE
H6700
L/CPL. G. BERZENSKI.
H6294. PTE. J. H. ADAMS.
H6771. PTE. P. J. ELLIS.
OF THE
WINNIPEG GRENADIERS
WHO DIED HAVING
DONE THEIR DUTY.
1942

Above: *This sign tells the grim story of the fate of the Canadian defenders of Hong Kong.*

Lt. Birkett's platoon encountered a battalion of infantry, and he was killed while protecting his men's retreat with a Bren gun. These small battles took place on 18-19 December. On the following day, a company of Grenadiers did reach the summit of Mount Butler and cleared it at bayonet point. Then the Japanese counterattacked and wiped out the Canadians or took them prisoner. During the company's last stand, Company Sergeant Major John Osborne threw himself on an enemy grenade, saving the lives of at least seven of his men, and winning a posthumous Victoria Cross. Meanwhile the Japanese overran Lawson's position, killing him and most of his officers.

The Japanese pressed the Canadians south, but at Sugarloaf Hill on 22 December soldiers under Major Bishop threw back the enemy. D Company of the Grenadiers held the Wong Nei Chong Gap until the same day, inflicting 800 casualties on the Japanese. Capt. R. W. Philip, his eye shot out, calmly put it in his pocket and went on directing the fighting. With all ammunition exhausted, he finally surrendered with 37 wounded men around him. The Japanese killed all those who could not walk.

On Christmas Day, D Company of the Rifles, ordered to attack Japanese positions at Stanley, charged down a narrow, open peninsula without artillery support. Despite the fire of light artillery, mortars, and machine guns from high ground, the Rifles reached Stanley Village and fought hand-to-hand with the Japanese. But then they fell back, after losing 104 men out of 148 – a 70 percent casualty rate.

On 25 December, after 17 and a half days of hard fighting, the troops in Hong Kong surrendered. The Japanese kept the survivors in Hong Kong until early 1943, and four officers and 123 other ranks died there. Four more were shot after trying to escape. Sent to Japan, the Canadians were slave labourers in coal and iron mines and 135 of them died.

As Canada's soldiers fought and died on Hong Kong, their Prime Minister sent them a message telling them that their bravery was 'an inspiration to us all' and adding that the country's 'name and its honour have never been more splendidly upheld.'

After the surrender, the Liberal government used a traditional device to mute any criticism. It appointed a Royal Commission, headed by the Chief Justice of Canada, Sir Lyman Duff, which held its hearings in secret. Released in June 1942, the report blamed no one for the disaster at Hong Kong, except the officer who failed to put C Force's vehicles on the ship that took the doomed men to defend the British colony.

Mackenzie King wrote to Duff, thanking him, and telling the judge that the report 'will help to give the people of Canada a confidence in their administration which means everything to this country's war effort.'

But the next time Canadians went into battle the results did nothing to create confidence in the government. And the country's losses were even greater than those in the disaster at Hong Kong.

met a Japanese patrol. He stood his ground as its members threw grenades, firing his Tommy gun. Together with another officer, he killed seven Japanese and the rest retreated. For his feat, the major won the Distinguished Service Order. His brave action was one of many in a hopeless battle.

Brigadier Lawson sent three platoons of Grenadiers to block a road junction and hold two crucial points – Jardine's Lookout and Mount Butler – as Japanese troops swept across the eastern side of the island. Lt. French's men found the Japanese already on Mount Butler, and failed to dislodge them. As they fell back, French died covering the withdrawal.

Dieppe

Tactically, it was an almost complete failure.
COL. C. P. STACEY, *The Canadian Army, 1939-1945* (1948)

Born in Verdun, Quebec in 1911, Bob Prouse lost his job when the company where he worked failed. After a spell with a detective agency, he joined the Canadian Provost Corps. Offered a choice in 1942 between training as an officer or taking part in a 'little manoeuvre coming up,' Prouse chose the second option.

And so he became a participant in 'Operation Jubilee,' the attack on the French port of Dieppe on 19 August 1942. Two commando forces and three Canadian groups landed in the early morning of that sunny day. By noon, Bob Prouse lay under a beached landing craft, shrapnel in his leg, a dead soldier nearby, watching his comrades being cut down by German fire as they retreated. He felt no fear – only a sense of detachment.

Then the firing stopped as the survivors of the manoeuvre that turned into a massacre surrendered. Bob Prouse's war ended at 1:30 p.m. – and then his sufferings as a German prisoner of war began. He called his reminiscences of his military career *Ticket to Hell – via Dieppe*. Prouse was one of 1946 Canadians captured by the Germans. Of the 2210 who made it back to England many were wounded, and 907 Canadians died. The Germans suffered 333 casualties, including 121 dead.

Below: *Dead soldiers, burning landing craft, and abandoned tanks tell the story of the Canadian raid on Dieppe on 19 August 1942.*

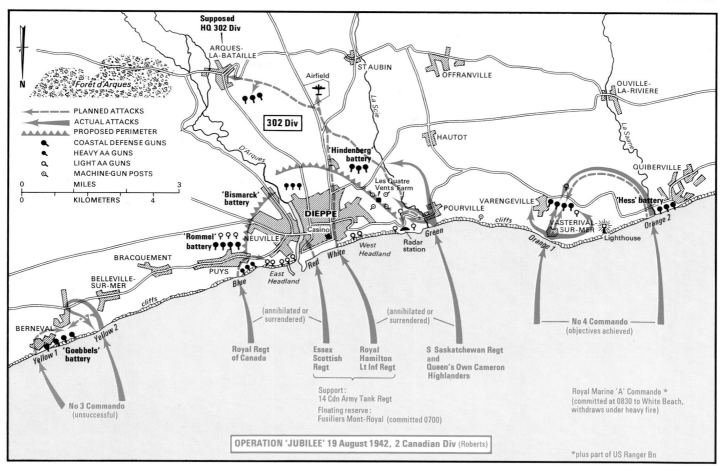

Map legend:

- ➤ PLANNED ATTACKS
- ➤ ACTUAL ATTACKS
- ◆◆◆ PROPOSED PERIMETER
- COASTAL DEFENSE GUNS
- HEAVY AA GUNS
- LIGHT AA GUNS
- MACHINE-GUN POSTS

MILES 0 — 3
KILOMETERS 0 — 4

Supposed HQ 302 Div
ARQUES-LA-BATAILLE
Forêt d'Arques
Airfield
ST AUBIN
OFFRANVILLE
OUVILLE-LA-RIVIERE
302 Div
La Scie
La Saane
HAUTOT
'Hindenberg' battery
QUIBERVILLE
D'Arques
'Bismarck' battery
Les Quatre Vents Farm
'Hess' battery
VARENGEVILLE
POURVILLE
DIEPPE
Casino
cliffs
STE-RIVAL-SUR-MER
Lighthouse
Orange 2
'Rommel' battery
NEUVILLE
West Headland
Radar station
Green
Orange 1
BRACQUEMENT
Red White
PUYS
Blue East Headland
BELLEVILLE-SUR-MER
cliffs
BERNEVAL
Yellow 2
Yellow 1
'Goebbels' battery

(annihilated or surrendered)   (annihilated or surrendered)

No 4 Commando (objectives achieved)

Royal Regt of Canada   Essex Scottish Regt   Royal Hamilton Lt Inf Regt   S Saskatchewan Regt and Queen's Own Cameron Highlanders

No 3 Commando (unsuccessful)

Support: 14 Cdn Army Tank Regt
Floating reserve: Fusiliers Mont-Royal (committed 0700)

Royal Marine 'A' Commando *
(committed at 0830 to White Beach, withdraws under heavy fire)

OPERATION 'JUBILEE' 19 August 1942, 2 Canadian Div (Roberts)

*plus part of US Ranger Bn

Above: *The Canadian landing at Dieppe.*

Overleaf: *German troops examine 'Bert,' one of the Calgary Regiment's tanks, after the Dieppe raid. Every Canadian tank was lost.*

The attack on Dieppe generated controversy as soon as the dazed survivors reached England. Prime Minister Winston Churchill defended it as 'an indispensable preliminary' to a full-scale invasion of France. The Outline Plan for Operation Jubilee, drawn up without Canadian participation, began:

Intelligence reports indicate that Dieppe is not heavily defended and that the beaches in the vicinity are suitable for landing Infantry, and Armoured Fighting Vehicles at some.

After three months of training, the Canadians embarked at 9:30 on the evening of 18 August. Their armada met a small German convoy at four on the following morning and fought a short battle with its escort. The air strike had been cancelled, and when the troops landed at Dieppe they took the defenders by surprise. But the Germans moved swiftly to man their guns as the soldiers swarmed ashore. The British No. 4 Commando quickly knocked out the German battery at Varengville, west of Dieppe, losing 12 men killed.

The three Canadian assaults turned into complete disasters.

The Royal Regiment came in under the cliffs at Puys, east of the town, as machine guns opened up on the landing craft. Then they sprayed the Canadians as they raced up the beach to the seawall, and hit them with mortar bombs while they tried to cut through barbed wire. Twenty soldiers reached the clifftop, but surrendered later. The battle on the beach at Puys ended at 8:30 a.m. One troop of German howitzers fired 550 rounds at the landing craft,

making evacuation impossible. Along the seawall and the beach lay 200 dead Royals, and only 65 members of the regiment returned to England.

The South Saskatchewan Regiment attacked at Pourville, drove up the valley of the Scie, and headed toward Dieppe. German fire killed scores of Canadians as they rushed a bridge over the river. Lt. Col. Cecil Merritt, the battalion commander, walked across the bridge, waving his helmet, oblivious to danger, and rallied his men. Then the Cameron Highlanders came ashore. Cheering on his men, their commander Lt. Col. Gostling leapt out of a landing craft – and died in a burst of fire. Flt. Sgt. Jack Nissen, a Cockney radar expert who settled in Canada after the war, went ashore with the South Saskatchewans to check out a German radar station on the cliffs beyond the Scie. He watched A Company of the South Saskatchewans slaughtered at the bridge – 'a tragedy that had to be seen to be understood.' Nissen recalls seeing Colonel Merritt, visibly aged, pale and drawn, fighting a rearguard action as the South Saskatchewans and the Camerons waded out to landing craft. With no chance of evacuation, the rearguard surrendered. Colonel Merritt received the Victoria Cross for his bravery at Dieppe.

The Royal Hamilton Light Infantry, the Essex Scottish and the Royal Marine Commando hit the beaches of Dieppe at 5:20 a.m. and surged forward, clearing pillboxes and strongpoints and capturing the beachfront casino. Then the Churchill tanks of the Calgary Regiment landed. Tracks spinning in the shingle, a few reached the seawall but could not

climb it. Bob Prouse pulled a wounded friend out of the way of the tanks, but watched a Churchill squash another soldier whose leg had been half blown off. The Calgary Regiment covered the infantry as it re-treated. But no tanks, and only one tank crew, re-turned to England.

Les Fusiliers Mont-Royal landed as reserves, but found they could not move off the beach. The retreat to the landing craft became general. One soldier claimed he made an Olympic runner look like a turtle. Darting across the bullet-swept shingle, Capt. J. W. Foote, chaplain of the Royal Hamiltons, treated wounded men and rescued others, carrying them to landing craft. He stayed with the men, and was captured by the Germans, becoming the first padre to win the Victoria Cross.

Operation Jubilee, too small for an invasion, too big for a raid, was planned to show the Americans and the Russians that an invasion of France in 1942 was not feasible, according to one theory. Jack Nis-sen's visit to Dieppe secured the knowledge needed to neutralize German radar. The military claimed that the lessons learned in the attack helped in plan-ning D-Day, the invasion of Europe on 6 June 1944. The cost of these lessons was high for Canada. One survivor, returning 40 years later, stood on the beach at Dieppe and said, 'We have no memorial and no marker here. The only thing we left on this beach was blood.'

Almost a year would pass before Canadians saw further action. Their next landing would stand in marked contrast to their baptism of fire in France.

Below: *Burying the dead of Dieppe, Brookwood Cemetery, Surrey, England, 23 August 1942. Maple leaves flown in from Canada were strewn on the coffins.*

Right: *The faces of defeat: A German soldier directs Canadian survivors of the Dieppe raid into captivity.*

Bottom right: *Wounded and weary, Canadians board a destroyer after the Dieppe raid.*

Italy

This war is so much like the last one, it's not even funny.
GENERAL HARRY CRERAR TO GENERAL L. E. M. BURNS, *Italy,*
(January 1944)

When 'Robbie' Robinson joined the West Nova Scotia Regiment in 1939, the doctor who examined him was the same one who had checked him when he enlisted for the First World War. In that war Robinson saw action at St. Eloi, Vimy and Passchendaele with the Royal Canadian regiment. When the West Novas landed in Sicily in July 1943, 'Robbie' went with them. Contrasting service in the two world wars, he said, 'In the first one, you could drive a man. In the second, you had to ask him if he would do something.'

The invasion of Italy gave Canadian soldiers their first taste of mobile warfare. Unable to command the skies over the Channel and so to safeguard an invasion of Britain, Hitler had turned eastward and invaded Russia on 22 June 1941. At first the panzers rolled ahead, cutting through the Russian Army, conquering vast tracts of territory. Meanwhile, General Rommel's Afrika Corps swept across North Africa. But Germany had overreached itself, and in 1942 the Allies counterattacked. Rommel, thrown back from the gates of Egypt at the Battle of El Alamein that began on 23 October, found his rear imperiled when the Allies landed in North Africa in early November. In that month the battle for Stalingrad in Russia began, and in February 1943 a complete German army surrendered there.

The invasion of Italy, aimed at knocking that country out of the war, tied down German divisions and relieved pressure on the Russians. The Germans chose the time and place of their stands, and built strongly defended lines across the Italian peninsula. The Canadian army played a major role in smashing through these lines. In sunny Italy,

Below: *Members of the 'Hasty Pees' (the Hastings and Prince Edward Regiment) advance on Nissoria, Sicily in July 1943.*

soldiers fought in the intense heat of summer, dust-choked and sweating, and froze in the winter, soaked by rain that churned the land to mud.

When the 1st Canadian Division and the 1st Canadian Army Tank Brigade landed with the 8th Army under General Bernard Montgomery in Sicily on 10 July 1943, it quickly secured its objective, Pachino airfield. Linking up with American troops, they pushed on to Assoro along narrow, winding roads defended by Germans fighting a skillful withdrawal action.

Assoro, like many Sicilian towns, stands on a 1000-metre-high hill. The commanding officer of the 'Hasty Pees' (The Hastings and Prince Edward Regiment) died while trying to determine the best way to attack the town. Major Lord Tweedsmuir, son of John Buchan, a former governor-general of Canada, took command, marching his men across country and up the mountain's steepest face. As 21 July dawned, the Hasty Pees stood near the castle of Assoro and proceeded to drive the Germans out. A German report stated that the Canadians had superior fieldcraft: 'Very mobile at night, surprise break-ins, clever infiltrations at night with small groups between our strongpoints.'

The Germans blew the bridge over a deep ravine that led to Leonforte, another hill town. On 21 July, the men of the Edmonton Regiment swarmed down the ravine and into the town while sappers rebuilt the bridge. Engaging the Germans in the dark narrow streets of Leonforte, the Edmontons received reinforcements from tanks and guns of the Princess Patricia's Canadian Light Infantry, and together they drove the Germans out of the town.

Three days later, the Royal Canadian Regiment took Nissoria. Beyond it lay two hills, and from here the Germans shelled the Canadians, killing the RCR's Commanding Officer, Lt. Col. Ralph Crowe. Mortar bombs wounded Major Tweedsmuir. His batman and two other men helped him down a hill, claiming the wounded officer was 'so full of lead he wouldn't float in molasses.' After taking Agira and Regalbuto, the Canadians probed into Adrano on 6 August, finding it empty. Then the Canadians moved into reserve and readied for the assault on the mainland of Italy.

Above: *Pvt M D White of the Edmonton Regiment takes cover behind a shell-blasted wall, Colle d'Anchise, 26 October 1943.*

Overleaf: *The attack on the German Gustav Line in central Italy. The Canadians formed part of General Montgomery's Eighth Army.*

Left: *General Bernard Montgomery speaks to Canadian troops in Sicily, July 1943.*

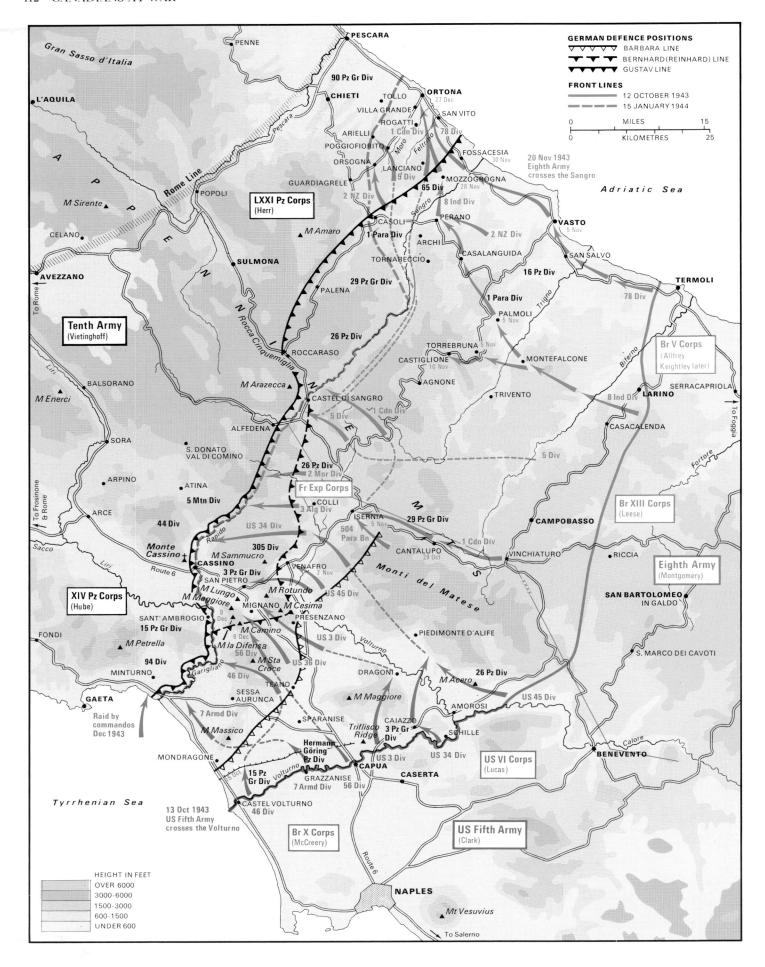

Gran Sasso d'Italia

PENNE

•PESCARA

90 Pz Gr Div

CHIETI

TOLLO

ORTONA
27 Dec

•L'AQUILA

VILLA GRANDE

ROGATTI

SAN VITO

ARIELLI

1 Cdn Div

78 Div

POGGIOFIORITO

ORSOGNA

LANCIANO
5 Div

FOSSACESIA
30 Nov

20 Nov 1943
Eighth Army
crosses the Sangro

GERMAN DEFENCE POSITIONS
∨∨∨∨ BARBARA LINE
∨▼∨▼ BERNHARD(REINHARD) LINE
▼▼▼ GUSTAV LINE

FRONT LINES
——— 12 OCTOBER 1943
– – – 15 JANUARY 1944

0   MILES   15
0   KILOMETRES   25

GUARDIAGRELE

MOZZOGROGNA
28 Nov

Adriatic Sea

LXXI Pz Corps
(Herr)

2 NZ Div

65 Div

8 Ind Div

Rome Line

POPOLI

CASOLI

PERANO

VASTO
5 Nov

M Sirente ▲

1 Para Div

ARCHI

CASALANGUIDA

SAN SALVO

CELANO •

TORNARECCIO

16 Pz Div

Tenth Army
(Vietinghoff)

SULMONA

29 Pz Gr Div

1 Para Div

PALMOLI
5 Nov

TERMOLI

AVEZZANO

PALENA

Trigno

78 Div

To Rome

TORREBRUNA 5 Nov

MONTEFALCONE

Br V Corps
(Allfrey
Keightley later)

BALSORANO

26 Pz Div

CASTIGLIONE
10 Nov

Biferno

SERRACAPRIOLA

M Enerci ▲

ROCCARASO

AGNONE

8 Ind Div

LARINO

To Foggia

SORA

M Arazecca ▲

TRIVENTO

CASALENDA

ARPINO

CASTEL DI SANGRO

1 Cdn Div

Fortore

ALFEDENA

5 Div

5 Div

S. DONATO
VAL DI COMINO

ATINA

26 Pz Div
2 Mor Div

Br XIII Corps
(Leese)

ARCE

5 Mtn Div

Fr Exp Corps

COLLI
3 Alg Div

ISERNIA
5 Nov

29 Pz Gr Div

CAMPOBASSO

RICCIA

44 Div

US 34 Div

504
Para Bn

1 Cdn Div

VINCHIATURO

Eighth Army
(Montgomery)

Rapido

305 Div

CANTALUPO
29 Oct

Monti del Matese

Monte
Cassino ✝

VENAFRO
2 Nov

SAN BARTOLOMEO
IN GALDO

Route 6

CASSINO

3 Pz Gr Div

M Sammucro ▲

M Rotundo

US 45 Div

XIV Pz Corps
(Hube)

SAN PIETRO

M Lungo

M Cesima

MIGNANO

PRESENZANO

S. MARCO DEI CAVOTI

M Maggiore

SANT'AMBROGIO

8
Dec

M Camino
6 Dec

US 3 Div

Volturno

PIEDIMONTE D'ALIFE

15 Pz Gr Div

M Petrella ▲

M la Difensa
56 Div

US 36 Div

26 Pz Div

94 Div

▲ M Sta
Croce

DRAGONI

M Acero

US 45 Div

MINTURNO

Garigliano

46 Div

TEANO

▲ M Maggiore

AMOROSI

GAETA

SESSA
AURUNCA

Triflisco
Ridge

CAIAZZO

3 Pz Gr
Div

SCHILLE

BENEVENTO

Raid by
commandos
Dec 1943

7 Armd Div

SPARANISE

Calore

M Massico ▲

Hermann
Göring
Pz Div

US 3 Div

US 34 Div

US VI Corps
(Lucas)

MONDRAGONE

15 Pz
Gr Div

Volturno

CAPUA

CASERTA

Tyrrhenian Sea

13 Oct 1943
US Fifth Army
crosses the Volturno

GRAZZANISE
7 Armd Div

56 Div

CASTEL VOLTURNO
46 Div

Br X Corps
(McCreery)

US Fifth Army
(Clark)

Route 6

HEIGHT IN FEET
OVER 6000
3000-6000
1500-3000
600-1500
UNDER 600

NAPLES

Mt Vesuvius ▲

To Salerno

Right: *A Sherman tank of the 1st Canadian Army Tank Brigade stirs up the summer dust of Regalbuto, 7 August 1943.*

Below: *The infantry bears the brunt of battle: Two wounded Canadians receive medical aid near Valguarnera, July 1943.*

Left: *A patrol of the Princess Patricia's Canadian Light Infantry strolls down the main street of Agira, July 1943.*

Right: *Where is the sniper? Members of the Carleton and York Regiment advance up an alley in Campochiaro under fire on 23 October 1943.*

Overleaf: *Diamond T tractor-trailers haul Sherman tanks of the 1st Canadian Army Tank Brigade near Manfredonia, 12 October 1943.*

Strome Galloway served with the Royal Canadian Regiment from its landing in Sicily to the fighting in Holland. Seconded to the London Irish in Tunisia, he was the only officer with combat experience when the RCR landed at Pachino. He recalls listening to Major Billy Pope, the battalion's second-in-command, asking the young officers if they had seen much of death in the sun. The major died attacking a tank at Valguarnera with an anti-tank weapon and a bomb he had forgotten to arm. Galloway describes some orders received by the battalion as 'criminal nonsense' and soon encountered some of the mindlessness of the military bureaucracy, receiving a consignment of lemons in the rations while surrounded by trees bearing this fruit.

Farley Mowat served with the Hasty Pees. He remembered the seasick men in the landing craft heading for the Sicilian shore; the shock of encountering the first dead enemy – an Italian lieutenant around his own age; the sheer fatigued numb-

ness of night marching; and the inedibility of the 'Compo' rations that contained a 12-ounce can of treacle pudding avidly sought by men starved of sweetstuffs. Mowat, bird-watching near Grammichele, suddenly found shells bursting nearby. He saw two Canadian weapons carriers 'brew up' as their gas tanks exploded. The soldiers made the acquaintance in Italy of the German '88,' which fired with a flat, sharp sound, and was 'a terrible gun if you were at the wrong end of it,' in the words of one man. After taking part in the attacks on Valguarnera and Assoro, Mowat went down with a bad case of dysentery, and was evacuated. The Hasty Pees reported 200 men killed, wounded, or missing in the Sicilian campaign. Total Canadian casualties for the three weeks came to 485 officers and men killed, and just under 2000 others wounded.

Before dawn on 3 September, the 1st Canadian Infantry Division boarded landing craft in Sicily and set out across the Straits of Messina to attack Reggio

di Calabria, on the toe of Italy's boot. The Italian troops they met soon surrendered, and the Germans withdrew northwards. The Hasty Pees advanced to Catanzaro in surrendered Italian trucks as the Canadians swept up the boot of Italy. American and British troops landed at Salerno on 9 September as General Eisenhower, the Allied supreme commander, announced an armistice with Italy.

The Canadians raced up the eastern coast of Italy, then swung into the Apennine Mountains running up the spine of the country and took the key town of Potenza. As they advanced, they experienced the characteristic German pattern of mountain fighting as the rains began and the weather turned cold. When the Canadians encountered heavy fire, they did not know whether it came from a German rearguard or if the enemy had dug in and intended to fight a prolonged action. From the central mountains, rivers run to the Adriatic, and the Canadians had to cross every one of them. Beyond the Sangro, midway up the peninsula, lay the town of Ortona. Beyond it lay the Winter Line, which connected with both the Hitler and Gustav lines on the western side of the Apennines.

By mid-November, the Canadians had a bridgehead across the Sangro. Then they crossed the Moro River. Near San Leonardo a platoon of the RCR turned a farmhouse into a fortress, killing 30 German attackers. Capt. Paul Triquet of the Van Doos, with a squadron from the Ontario Tank Regiment, led his men up a mine-thick, muddy gully to capture Casa Berardi. He reached his objective with only 17 soldiers and four tanks, and held it against repeated German counterattacks, winning the first Victoria Cross of the Mediterranean campaign.

Just before Christmas 1943, the Canadians reached the port of Ortona in front of the Winter Line. Here began one of the bloodiest battles of the Italian campaign. The German paratroopers defended the town with great tenacity, and the Edmontons and the Seaforth Highlanders took it street by street, house by house. The Canadians perfected the technique of 'mouse-holing,' moving from house to house by blasting gaps in the connecting walls. The 75-mm guns of the Trois Rivières Regiment smashed the Germans out of their positions.

The battle for Ortona went on through Christmas Day. In a captured church, the weary Seaforths of the rifle companies moved through in rotation. They sat down to their Christmas dinner served on a white tablecloth, while the pipe major made music and a signals officer played carols on the organ. After a two-hour break from war, the soldiers went back to killing – and being killed. The 1st Brigade, attempting to outflank the enemy, pushed through mire, mines and rain to take the high ground north of Ortona. Cut off, the soldiers went hungry on Christmas Day when supplies failed to reach them. Strome Galloway described the attack on Ortona as 'a walk into catastrophe.' Mortars and machine guns left the RCR with a fighting strength of 18 officers and 159 men. Galloway wished a grimly-smiling Cpl. J. E.

Morton luck as he trudged forward with his Bren gun into a vineyard. The man's brother had died in the assault on Assoro, and minutes later he too lay dead.

Like Galloway, Farley Mowat expresses contempt for the higher command and the paper pushers behind the lines. One major chased Mowat for an accounting of the mess funds, which showed a small discrepancy. Mowat pointed out that the accounts, and the previous mess secretary, had been blown to bits by a landmine. The pompous officer merely stated that copies should have been kept in a safe place.

Mowat's youthful idealism had turned sour and savage as the Hasty Pees fought their way up Italy. He survived when his truck, carrying three-inch mortar bombs, ran over a mine. In Ferrazzano a German sprayed Mowat's back with a Schmeisser machine pistol. The bullets hit tins of bully beef that Mowat had stowed there to trade with the local residents. In crossing the Moro River in December 1943, the Hasty Pees lost a third of its 400 men killed or wounded.

After Ortona fell, the Canadian troops settled into three months of warfare similar to that on the Western Front in the First World War, as the 8th Army's offensive ground to a halt. The landscape became waterlogged and the roads covered in 'chocolate sauce,' vehicles unable to move off them. As troops hunkered down in slit trenches full of water, temperatures at night fell below freezing. A favourite joke became, 'Come to Sunny Italy for your holiday.' The Germans held the high ground and shot at anything that moved. So the Canadians slept in mud and misery during the day, becoming active as night fell. Patrols went out, the men squirming through mud on their bellies, trying to avoid 'S' mines that exploded in showers of ball bearings, freezing when flares went up, alert to the chatter of machine guns and the thump of mortars. The soldiers sought prisoners or a better understanding of enemy positions.

Early in 1944, the Allies made a drive for Rome. The Americans established a bridgehead at Anzio south of the city on 22 January, but failed to break out of it. To the south, Allied troops tried to take Cassino and Monastery Hill above it, the key points in the Gustav and Hitler lines. At 11 p.m. on 11 May, 1000 guns opened up on the Gustav Line. The 1st Canadian Armoured Division supported Indian infantry and crossed the Gari River to engage the enemy. The Commonwealth troops broke the Gustav Line. The 1st Canadian Infantry Division relieved the Indians on 16 May and attacked the Hitler Line in the Liri Valley. The Ontario Regiment lost 13 tanks in one assault, but the Canadians failed to breach the Hitler Line. They held their positions while 400 artillery pieces rained shells on the enemy clinging to the rocks and crags facing them for three days.

On 23 May, 800 guns fired on the enemy, and at 6 a.m. the Canadian assault battalions attacked. The Seaforths reached their objective by mid-morning, but the Princess Pat's, pinned down by a hail of fire,

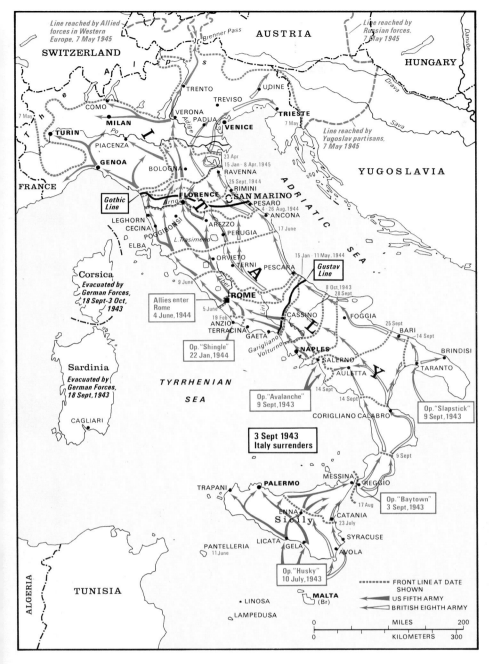

Left: *A mortar crew of the Saskatoon Light Infantry in action at Ortona on 5 January 1944.*

Above: *The Allied advance through Italy.*

position, and received the Victoria Cross for his bravery. Perkins won the Distinguished Service Order.

In the attack in the Liri Valley, as Major W. de N. Watson, commander of A Company of the Princess Pat's, advanced toward his objective, every one of his men became a casualty. Wounded twice, he settled into a 'large and comfortable shell hole,' and during the night reconnoitred his objective. Finding it still held by the enemy, he went to ground and, a day later, the regiment's War Diary recorded he was located 'near an 88-mm gun, suffering from a wound in one arm, a piece off his helmet and a Schmeisser bullet in his forehead, and a tremendous appetite.'

Rome fell on 4 June 1944, two days before D-Day in Normandy. The Germans, outflanked, abandoned the Winter Line and moved 300 kilometres north to the next line of fortifications – the Gothic Line, stretching from north of Pisa to just south of Rimini. Beyond that line lay open country and the valley of the Po, where swift movement and rapid deployment of armour would be possible.

To reach the Adriatic Front, Canadian engineers improved mountain tracks through the central mountains in seven days. Canadian tanks and troop carriers rumbled through the mountains and took up positions before the Gothic Line. Here Panther tanks sat in concrete bunkers, reinforced dugouts housed machine guns covering every approach, and anti-tank ditches and barbed wire lay in wait.

At 10:35 p.m. on 25 August, four battalions of the 1st Canadian Infantry Division crossed the Matauro River as artillery opened up on the German positions. The enemy had fled from their front line positions, but the Canadians had to clear them from broken ground in front of the Gothic Line. They crossed yet another river, the Foglia, dying in its mine-sown flats. In the early morning of 1 September, the Princess Louise Dragoon Guards suffered 129 casualties while assaulting a commanding German position, but they took it.

The weather broke as Canadian infantry and armour advanced toward Rimini. Attacking the airfield there, Strome Galloway of the RCR set up battalion headquarters in a farmhouse. Outside it lay a dead German paratrooper. His pockets contained three printed death notices on his brothers, all volunteers, all winners of the Iron Cross. Snapshots showed the happy family together in their home town of Zweibrucken, from which Galloway's mother's ancestors had come to Canada 200 years earlier. He wrote that he was 'never a German-hater,' and that very few fighting men were.

The Canadians took the bastions of San Martino and San Fortunato overlooking Rimini, and could see to the north the plains of Romagna reaching to the horizon. The fall rains and German explosives had turned this low-lying land into a swamp. On 20 October, the Princess Pat's established a bridgehead beyond the Savio River where the Edmontons and Seaforths joined them. As a forward company of the Seaforths dug in, three Panther tanks, two self-

could not move. Then the Seaforths came under attack from German tanks. On the left flank the Carleton and York Regiment fought through while the 51st Royal Tank Regiment battled German tanks and anti-tank gunners. Then the West Novas joined the battle, advancing past the burning hulks of Churchill tanks to wipe out German pillboxes. Shortly after dawn on 24 May, tanks of the 5th Canadian Armoured Division rolled through the gap in the Hitler Line. In one day's fighting, the Canadians lost 60 tanks and suffered 889 casualties.

In the Battle of the Melfa River, Lt. E. J. Perkins of the Strathconas took his light tanks across the river, where Major J. K. Mahony joined him with a company of the Westminster Regiment. They held the bridgehead against repeated German counter-attacks. Mahony lost half his men and became the focus of German fire. Wounded once in the head and twice in the leg, Mahony stubbornly held the

Left: *A Canadian patrol searches for enemy machine gun nests in the coastal resort of Rimini.*

Bottom left: *Cape Breton Highlanders disembark from the SS* Monterey *at Naples on 10 November 1943, to the sound of bagpipes.*

propelled guns and a platoon of infantry counter-attacked. Private Ernest Smith hit one tank with a PIAT (Projector, Infantry, Anti-Tank), killed four Germans and drove the rest back. Protecting a wounded comrade, Smith fought off another tank, and won the Victoria Cross.

Fred Cederberg served with the Cape Breton Highlanders in Italy. He describes vividly how the war looked from the slit trenches in which he and his friend cowered, alert to every threatening movement. His first action at the Arielli River in December had been a fiasco. Fired on by British soldiers who mistook them for Germans, the assault companies had flopped face down in the mud and water where the enemy mortared them. The survivors withdrew in the darkness, and their colonel spoke to them as they counted their 13 dead and 33 wounded. 'Nobody stops for the men who've been hit,' he said. 'No attack can succeed unless you keep moving.' The green men listened, shocked. Cederberg, a sergeant, drew around him a small group of men who looked out for each other. A sudden shower of mortar shells fell among them. One tore off the arm of a friend, and they shouted for a stretcher bearer. But it was too late; the man's life had bled away. A shell obliterated another soldier, but they did not mourn him: 'He was a stranger. They hardly knew him.'

Platoon members went after prisoners, lured by the promise of a medal, $50 and a week's leave if they captured one. They managed to do so, but missed the reward. One man took the prisoner back, but he broke away, ran into a minefield and died there. On another occasion they ambushed a German patrol. An officer raised a white flag, and asked for permission to recover the dead and wounded. Cederberg

gave it – and also lent the Germans stretchers and morphine. They returned them after the truce – with a bottle of schnapps.

The Highlanders moved forward toward the Senio in the fall of 1944. Rocket-firing Typhoons aided their advance. And a new weapon helped a company of Westminsters cross the Munio Canal on 16 December. 'Wasps,' flame-throwing carriers, shrivelled the German machine gunners on the far bank.

But still the Germans fought on. Cederberg tells of replacements coming into the line. He had trained artillerymen to become infantry as Canadian losses mounted, teaching them that their shovel was their key to survival – not their weapon. Cederberg urged a new arrival to dig a deep slit trench. He did not, and after a shelling was found sliced in half.

By Christmas Day, the Canadians had reached the banks of the Senio, and observed a wary truce with the Germans. Both sides had reached a limit beyond which men could not go. Cederberg's platoon should have had 32 men. It had seven. An officer wrote of the lull before returning to 'the cold reality of war and all its ugliness.' The men 'became human again and war seemed far away, almost forgotten.' In January, troops from British Columbia, Ontario and Cape Breton cleared the Germans from around Cotignola and the Valli di Comacchio, a vast lagoon.

The poplars still shade the roads of the Romagna plain, and the fruitful flat landscape dozes in the sun, showing no sign of the bitter battles fought over it. Of the 92,757 Canadians who served in Italy, a quarter became casualties. And 5799 of them still lie in Italian soil.

Right: *In the winter cold of 'sunny Italy,' tanks of the 5th Canadian Armoured Brigade advance through Ravenna on 12 January 1945.*

D-Day and Northwest Europe

The average Canadian soldier is reasonable, sensible and
has the independence and initiative to become difficult if
he considers he is being treated unreasonably.
REPORT OF MAJ. R. A. GREGORY, NEURO-PSYCHIATRIST,
3 CDN. INF. DIV. (October 1944)

While the Canadians in Italy dug in along the Senio to wait out the winter, their comrades-in-arms stood ready for the final effort that would end the war in 1945.

The first Canadians to land in France in 1944 were members of the 1st Canadian Parachute Battalion, who jumped into action on the night before D-Day, 6 June. In the invasion, the 3rd Canadian Division had been assigned to Juno Beach, an 8 kilometre stretch of Normandy coast between Bernières-sur-Mer and Courseulles-sur-Mer. Securing the beachhead, the 15,000 Canadian and 9000 British troops of the division would thrust inland and capture the Caen-Bayeux road and Carpiquet airfield, about 20 kilometres from the coast, by nightfall. It took them three weeks.

Coming in through choppy seas and strong currents, the landing craft had to avoid reefs, rocks, and 14,000 mines sown by the Germans. The advance became a series of bloody battles against strong Panzer groups, including the 12th S.S. Division commanded by General Kurt Meyer and made up of fanatical Hitler Youth directed by experienced officers and noncommissioned officers who had served on the Russian Front. The Canadians suffered 1074 casualties on D-Day, including 359 dead.

Ben Dunkleman, a mortar platoon commander with the Queen's Own Rifles, had become sick and tired of 'training and retraining, and of running all over England in the rain.' Now pitching and rolling in a landing craft, Dunkleman felt awe-stricken at the sky above him black with aircraft and the sea thick with warships. The assault companies climbed the seawalls and charged the machine guns and 88s raking the beach. One company lost half its members, and advanced under the command of a corporal. Rough seas prevented Canadian vehicles from landing but finally they came ashore. The engineers blew great holes in the seawall, and the tanks and weapon carriers went inland, backing up the assault companies.

Dunkleman watched in horror as tanks carrying infantry charged straight at the enemy. The German Tiger tanks completely outgunned the Canadian Shermans which the enemy referred to as 'the Ronson lighter' – one spark and it lit up. Many of the tanks 'brewed up' as the 88s hit them, and few of the infantry survived. Dunkleman aimed his mortars, armed with phosphorous bombs, at nearby haystacks which he suspected concealed tanks. His hunch proved correct. As the stacks caught fire, tank crews

Above: *A landing craft takes troops ashore from HMCS* Prince David *to Bernières-sur-Mer in Normandy on D-Day, 6 June 1944.*

Top right: *Troops of the 9th Canadian Infantry Division struggle ashore at Bernières-sur-Mer on D-Day.*

Right: *Wrecked vehicles off the invasion beaches on D-Day. Despite the less-than-favourable weather conditions, almost all the landing force reached the beaches without mishap.*

Left: Tanks of the 1st Hussars and troops of the Royal Winnipeg Rifles and the Regina Rifles land near Courseulles-sur-Mer on D-Day.

Right: A dead Canadian soldier lies in front of a German pillbox (left), somewhere on the Normandy coast, four days after D-Day.

Below: A map of the D-Day landings, showing the location of the invasion beaches. The Canadians went ashore at Juno Beach.

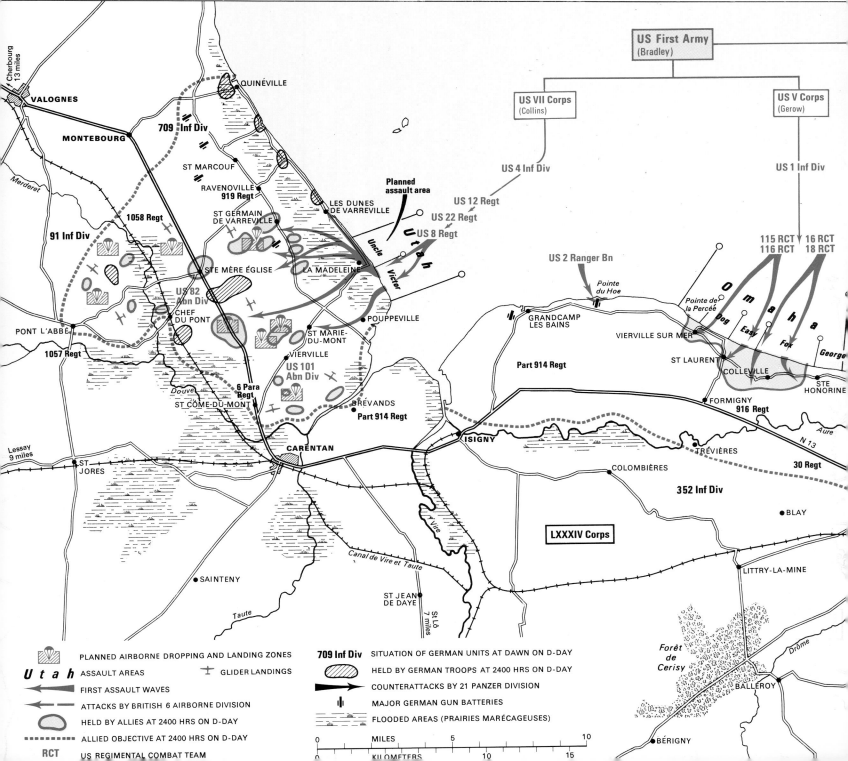

PLANNED AIRBORNE DROPPING AND LANDING ZONES

Utah ASSAULT AREAS   ⊤ GLIDER LANDINGS

FIRST ASSAULT WAVES

ATTACKS BY BRITISH 6 AIRBORNE DIVISION

HELD BY ALLIES AT 2400 HRS ON D-DAY

ALLIED OBJECTIVE AT 2400 HRS ON D-DAY

RCT   US REGIMENTAL COMBAT TEAM

709 Inf Div SITUATION OF GERMAN UNITS AT DAWN ON D-DAY

HELD BY GERMAN TROOPS AT 2400 HRS ON D-DAY

COUNTERATTACKS BY 21 PANZER DIVISION

MAJOR GERMAN GUN BATTERIES

FLOODED AREAS (PRAIRIES MARÉCAGEUSES)

0   MILES   5   10

0   KILOMETERS   10   15

bailed out. Then an Indian scout with the Regina Rifles pointed to a German helmet 1500 metres away. Dunkleman had trouble seeing it with his binoculars, but quickly called for a mortar barrage. Hundreds of Germans broke cover and began to run in all directions. Following the retreating Panzers, Dunkleman was blown out of his carrier, his uniform ablaze. By this time, one company of the Queen's Own had lost 100 out of its 135 men. And while on patrol, Dunkleman came across grim evidence of the work of the 12th S.S. Panzer Division. Canadian soldiers captured in the battle near Authie were shot, bayoneted and run over by tanks. At his trial for these atrocities, Meyer claimed that he had seen Germans, including wounded, shot down in cold blood, and that the Canadians had orders to take no prisoners.

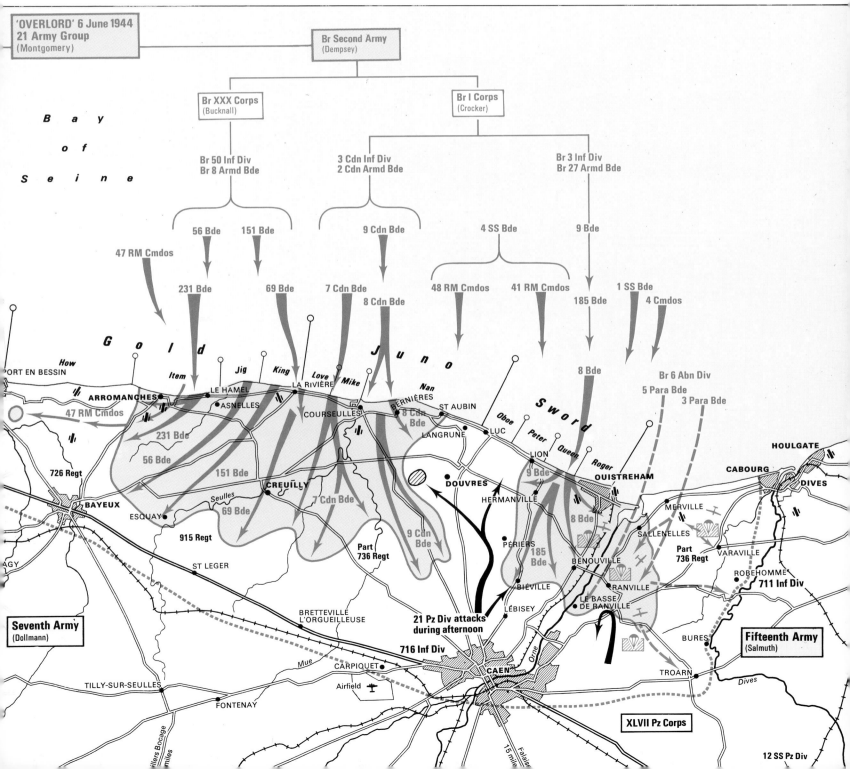

The fierceness of the fighting in Normandy, and the initial enthusiasm of Canadian soldiers for battle, emerges from the War Diary of the Canadian Scottish for 8 June. As they advanced, Cpl. Bob Mayfield said, 'Boy, this is going to be one hell of a good scrap!' The diary adds, 'It was questionable whether the men were more human or devil at this stage.' The Diary mentions three men who sprayed the enemy with a Bren gun from the hip, 'laughing gleefully as they did so.'

Caen, bombed into oblivion, fell on 10 July. The Americans, swinging west then south, moved around to trap the enemy forces confronting the Canadians and the British as they advanced on Falaise. Attacking on 25 July, the Canadian Black Watch suffered many casualties, including their commanding officer, Lt. Col. S. S. T. Cantlie, in clearing St. Martin. Major F. P. Griffin took over, leading four rifle companies toward Fontenay. The men came under fire from Germans dug in on Verrières Ridge which lay across their line of advance. The battalion had been in France for only two weeks, but charged the ridge like veterans. Here they encountered tanks disguised as haystacks, and could advance no further. Griffin ordered his men to return to their own lines, but only 15 did so. On that day, the Black Watch lost 307 men, including 123 killed. When Verrières Ridge fell on 8 August, Major Griffin lay dead among his men.

On the night before, Operation Totalize had begun with Bomber Command and strong artillery support smashing the Germans, and the Canadians advanced towards Falaise. Here they would link up with the Americans and trap the Germans. The enemy fought desperately to escape the closing jaws of the trap.

On 19 August, Major D. V. Currie took the village of St. Lambert-sur-Dives with a small detachment from the 4th Canadian Armoured Division and stopped many Germans from escaping from the Falaise killing ground. With 175 men he held off German counterattacks for four days until relieved, and captured 2000 enemy soldiers. Major Currie received the first Victoria Cross of the campaign in northwest Europe. The Canadians had used self-propelled guns, known as 'priests,' in the advance. As they advanced, they created 'unfrocked priests' by removing the guns and turning the vehicles into Armoured Personnel Carriers.

Only 300 members of the 20,000-strong 12th S.S. Panzer Division escaped from the Falaise trap. Kurt Meyer made it out on foot. After the war he was tried by a court martial headed by Major General Harry Foster, and sentenced to death. Reprieved, he later advised the Canadian army on defending the Alaska Highway against the Russians – while serving time in Dorchester Penitentiary!

With Paris liberated on 25 August, the Canadians

Left: *Canadian troops in the ruined French city of Caen on 10 July 1944.*

Below: *The advance into France: The 3rd Canadian Division moves on Bretteville-le-Rabet, 14 August 1944.*

Above: *Members of the 7th Canadian Infantry Brigade with a German prisoner at Authie, 9 July 1944.*

Above: *Major Currie supervises the roundup of German prisoners at St Lambert-sur-Dives, where he won the Victoria Cross, on 19 August 1944.*

Left: *Canadian tanks in the mud near Putte, Netherlands, 6 October 1944.*

Right: *Canadian troops fought through this waterlogged land south of Bergen-op-Zoom to open the port of Antwerp, November 1944.*

entered Rouen five days later after routing strong German forces from the nearby forest. On 1 September, the Canadian Hussars reached Dieppe, where crowds of residents blocked the street to welcome them. In August, the 1st Canadian Army suffered 9368 casualties, a quarter of them killed in action or dying of wounds. It had been, as the title of one book on the campaign put it, a 'bloody victory.'

The Canadians swung down the French coast, covering the long left flank of the Allied armies, taking the coastal ports. Dunkleman's company

Below: Pvt L R Decatsye *of the Highland Light Infantry of Canada catches up with the news in a foxhole in France, 20 June 1944.*

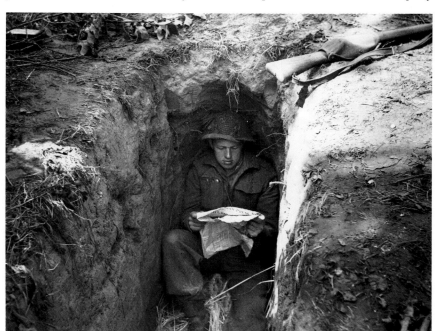

commander died before Boulogne, which took five days to reduce. Dunkleman recalled that by then, 'we lived like animals.' Sustained by rum, they crouched in flooded slit trenches to escape the enemy shelling. Dunkleman recalled the surrender of Boulogne in late September. A corporal, wearing a silk hat and playing 'The Skater's Waltz' on a 'liberated' violin, led out a string of prisoners. 'Perhaps we were all temporarily insane,' Dunkleman wrote in his memoirs.

As the Regina Rifles advanced on coastal guns near St. Inglevert, they opened up on them. Greg Clark's son Murray, a lieutenant, threw himself into a sunken road, landing on a mine. It set off the phosphorous bombs he carried, and he died in searing flames.

The Allies had captured the great Belgian port of Antwerp intact on 4 September. It lay 80 kilometres from the sea, and could be used to supply the advancing army. But the way to the port lay under German guns. Field Marshal Montgomery ordered the Canadians to clear the banks of the Scheldt River – without adequate support. Then he turned to direct his masterstroke to divide Germany from Holland, and end the war before the end of the year. 'Operation Market Garden' ended with the failure of airborne troops to take the one 'bridge too far' at Arnhem.

By destroying dikes and flooding the reclaimed land, the Germans had turned the land between Antwerp and the North Sea into a morass bisected by long causeways which they commanded with their guns. The 2nd Canadian Infantry Division went into battle against heavy German opposition. The Black

Watch reported a part of C Company killed or taken prisoner, and A Company 'slaughtered' and reduced to nine men. Reinforcements with little or no infantry training showed poor morale. Some crawled into haystacks and stayed there until the action ended. As one intelligence officer wrote, 'Against tough, seasoned enemy paratroopers, these reinforcements were more of a liability than an asset.' In wet, cold weather, with floods rising and high winds, the Canadians took Woensdrecht on 16-21 October, opening the way to Beveland and the causeway linking South Beveland to Walcheren Island.

Brigade Major George Hees led a group of Calgary Highlanders across the causeway, past a crater blown in the middle of it by the retreating Germans, and was wounded in the arm. He survived to become a Member of Parliament, and a popular and effective Minister of Veterans' Affairs.

The Royal Air Force bombed the dikes around Walcheren Island, the Canadians attacked by land over the causeway, other troops came in over the water, and the island fell. Meanwhile the Canadians had cleared the Breskens pocket south of Walche-

ren, attacking across the Leopold Canal while 'Wasps' spat flame at the far bank. The Canadian Scottish crossed the canal without opposition, but a platoon of the Royal Montreal Regiment was almost wiped out by enemy fire. Lt. Barclay rallied the men to the water's edge, coolly and efficiently, and then died in a burst of machine gun fire as his boat reached the bank. Beyond the canal, the Canadians fought from dike to dike. One company of the Queen's Own Rifles, reduced to two platoons, crawled to within 300 metres of enemy positions near Oostburg. Lt. E. J. Boos ordered them to fix bayonets, and they charged the enemy and captured the entrance to the town without casualties. Lt. Boos received the Military Cross.

Between 1 October and 8 November, the Canadians lost 355 officers and 6012 men. When an Allied convoy led by the Canadian-built *Fort Cataraqui* sailed into Antwerp on 28 November to a special ceremony marking the opening of the Scheldt, no one bothered to invite a representative of the Canadian army.

Meanwhile, at home, the heavy losses sustained

Below: *A field artillery tractor slides off the road near the Beveland Canal, Netherlands, on 28 October 1944.*

Right: *Canada's unlikely war leader: Prime Minister Mackenzie King, seen here with his dog Pat.*

Below: *A gun crew of the 5th Field Regiment, Royal Canadian Artillery, in action at Molden, Netherlands, 1 February 1945.*

by that army induced the government to introduce conscription, and to send men who were not volunteers into battle. Previously all Canadians serving overseas had been volunteers. Other soldiers had been conscripted only to defend North America. Some had gone to invade Kiska in the fog-shrouded Aleutian Islands, occupied by the Japanese in 1942. But when the invasion fleet reached the island in August 1943, the Japanese had fled. On 22 November 1944, Prime Minister Mackenzie King announced that men conscripted under the National Resources Mobilization Act would go overseas. In all, 12,908 conscripts served overseas, with 2500 reaching the front lines. They suffered 315 casualties, including 69 deaths.

A painting by Alex Colville shows Canadian soldiers walking along a dike near Nijmegen. It is impossible to tell whether they are heading into combat, or moving away from it after being relieved. Led by a corporal, they are tired, weary, their eyes closed, walking like dead men. An infantryman who fought in northwest Europe calculated that a Canadian footslogger in that campaign in 1944-45

stood a greater chance of becoming a 'battle casualty' than did his father during an equivalent period on the Western Front in the First World War. In 1914-18, battalions had an average of 100 casualties a month. In 1944-45, casualties averaged 175 a month.

By the end of 1944, while the Canadian army waited to take part in the final assault over the Rhine and into Germany, its ranks contained battle-hardened veterans and nervous replacements for those killed and wounded, awaiting their first action. In October, Major R. A. Gregory, a neuro-psychiatrist, reported that 15 percent of all casualties during the Battle of the Scheldt suffered from 'neuro-psychiatric' problems, most of them after three months in combat. He suggested that in this theatre of war 'a man may retain good efficiency from 18-21 days without rest.' After that, morale declined and soldiers lost their volition. Gregory recommended a short change, and that men be sent back to the leave center in Brussels for 24 to 48 hours 'of carefree living' before going back into battle.

On 8 February 1945, 'Operation Veritable' began as the 1st Canadian Army, the largest ever commanded by a Canadian officer, rolled toward the Reichswald. Bombers smashed German communications centers beyond the boundary between the Netherlands and Germany, artillery fired 160,000 shells, tanks rumbled forward, and support aircraft blasted targets on the ground. The Germans fell back, and again the Canadians found themselves in flooded land. The Princess Patricia's, driving down the west bank of the Rhine through pouring rain, laughed at signs saying, 'Dust draws shells.' Armour bogged down in the wet land was picked off by German 88s. The Germans fought hard for Moyland Wood near Cleve. On the evening of 19 February, a company of Canadian Scottish thwarted six German counterattacks on their positions.

The Canadians jumped aboard tanks and 'Kangaroos' (Armoured Personnel Carriers), dropping off to attack German positions. On the road between Calcar and Udem, Sgt. Aubrey Cosens of the Queen's Own Rifles won the V.C. His officer dead and the platoon reduced to four men and himself, Cosens directed the fire of a tank at German positions and then broke an enemy counterattack. Riding on the tank, he ordered it to ram an enemy-held building, then dropped off, cleared the building and attacked several more, killing 20 Germans and capturing many others. Setting up defences, he went to report to his company commander, only to be killed by a sniper.

The Canadians advanced to the Hochwald, heavily mined by the enemy. Ben Dunkleman recalled being roused at 3:30 a.m. and wondering whether he would ever see another morning. The Canadians advanced under artificial moonlight, and by the end of 'that gruesome day' he had only 36 fighting men in his company out of 115 who had followed him into the attack.

A few days later, Dunkleman ordered a tank commander to move ahead of his infantry, but the man refused, despite a threat to shoot him. Dunkleman called his men together and asked for suggestions on how to cross the mine-strewn land ahead of them. They suggested that no one would lay mines near trees, so they jumped from tree to tree across the forest. For his courage and leadership in the Hochwald, Dunkleman was awarded the Distinguished Service Order.

Left: *Infantrymen of the Regiment de Mont Royal flush out German soldiers in Groningen, Netherlands, 15 April 1945.*

Right: *A Sherman tank of the South Alberta Regiment, spare tracks on its hull for extra protection, waits to go into battle near Calcar, Germany, on 26 February 1945.*

Major F. A. Tilston of the Essex Scottish won the Victoria Cross there. Wounded again and again, with his company down to a quarter of its original strength, he fought off counterattacks. The Canadians took Veen on 9 March, a town with houses built to be turned into pillboxes.

On 23 March 1945, 'Operation Plunder' began with the roar of 1300 guns firing across the Rhine. The Highland Light Infantry of Canada crossed the river on the following morning and attacked Speldrop. A private reported that they began house and barn clearing at the edge of the town, adding that, 'Not many prisoners were taken, as if they did not surrender before we started, they never had the opportunity afterwards.' The 1st Canadian Parachute Battalion dropped near Wessel and lost their commander, Lt. Col. J. A. Nicklin, in the assault. Cpl. F. G. Topham, a medical orderly who had been hit in the face, dressed the wounds of a soldier in the open, then carried him to safety under fire. Refusing evacuation, Topham rescued three men from a burning ammunition carrier, and won the last V.C. of the campaign. The 'paras,' the first to land in Europe, took Minden, crossed the Elbe, and headed for the shores of the Baltic at Wismar, making the deepest penetration into Germany of any of the Allied troops.

The 1st Canadian Division, transferred from Italy, captured the ghost town of Arnhem. The Allies learned that people in western Holland, reduced to eating bulbs for food, were dying in their hundreds from starvation. A truce was called, and food supplies trucked in and dropped from the air.

A Dutch woman recalled the liberation of her town in April by Canadians, and six tired soldiers who had been on the go for 40 hours without a break standing outside her house. They smiled when the Dutch called them 'Tommies,' and explained that they were Canadians. The woman agreed to take them in, and soon machine guns, rifles, shovels, hand grenades, steel helmets, and kit bags rendered her house unrecognizable. One soldier, of Belgian descent, showed her a picture of his wife and two children, and a 19-year-old showed her a photo of his girlfriend.

Two other soldiers shared their food with the family and took the children to the cookhouse. On the following morning, they shaved, singing, punching and kidding one another. The Dutch family felt completely at home with them. In the evening the troops learned they had to be ready to leave in five minutes. Some slept, while others chatted with the family. 'All of them were afraid,' the woman wrote. When they left on the next morning, they showed little warmth as they said goodbye, asking their hosts to keep their fingers crossed.

Two months later, a corporal arrived at the woman's home. It was one of the Canadian soldiers. The woman said that she had not expected to see any of them again, because they had gone off with scarcely a goodbye. The soldier said simply, that, 'One gets fed up with saying goodbyes.' As the Dutch woman put it, 'They had felt just as hopeless

Left: *Members of the first Canadian Women's Army Corps contingent to enter Germany, June 1945.*

Below: *The military in Halifax, Nova Scotia, celebrated victory in Europe by rioting on 8 May 1945.*

Below right: *Prime Minister Mackenzie King and Louis St Laurent address the nation on VE Day.*

Bottom right: *A Canadian Repatriation Depot in Thursley, England, 22 May 1945.*

and helpless' as she had as they left. One soldier had been killed by a sniper, and three others had been badly wounded by a shell. Only one remained un-wounded, and he had spent six weeks in hospital with a nervous rash. He said, 'Well, I guess I'm no hero.' Yet he had gone out under fire to see if he could succour his friends.

The end of the Second World War in Europe came with Canadian troops still out front, pushing ahead. On 4 May, General Crerar, commander of all Canadian soldiers, told his subordinates to cease attacking. The German surrender became effective at 8 a.m. on the following morning. On 8 May, Field Marshal Montgomery wrote to General Crerar, thanking him for all he had done, and stating that under his command, 'magnificent Canadian soldiers' had covered themselves with glory.

Generals Foulkes and Simonds, the two Canadian Corps commanders, accepted the surren-der of the German forces in their sector. One enemy general, shaken at learning how young his opponents

were, received a further shock when he learned that Brigadier J. A. Roberts, commander of the 8th Canadian Infantry Brigade, had been a manufac-turer before the war, not a regular soldier.

The Canadian Army began as a group of amateurs who became highly skilled and professional in the crucible of war. They fought and defeated tough, skilled, experienced German regulars. But the price of their learning came high. From D-Day to VE Day, Canadians had suffered just under 48,000 casual-ties, including 12,579 dead.

Just before he died, on 25 June 1986, Major David Currie said modestly that most people did not know about his Victoria Cross. But he saw nothing wrong with that. 'Why should they?' he asked. 'It's a long time since the war. It's over the hill.' George Hees, returning to Holland for a celebration honoring vet-erans in May 1985, also showed characteristic Canadian modesty at their reception. 'They make us feel like delivering angels. It's almost embarrassing. We just did our job,' he said.

IN THE AIR

. . . throughout my operations I never hated a single
German, and had no hatred for them as a people.
WALTER THOMPSON, *Lancaster to Berlin* (1985)

In the spring of 1941, 17-year-old Murray Peden attended a recruiting rally in Winnipeg addressed by Billy Bishop. Impressed by the Canadian ace's pugnaciousness, dignity and daring, Peden and his friend Rod Dunphy vowed to become fighter pilots. They served instead in Bomber Command. Dunphy died over Frankfurt on 20 December 1943. A lake near Lynn Lake in Manitoba is named after him. Peden became a pilot, surviving 30 missions to write one of the classic accounts of the air offensive against Germany - *A Thousand Shall Fall.*

Canadian airmen fought in the Battle of Britain, and 10,000 of them fell while serving with Bomber Command. On the night of 24-25 March 1944, 545 aircrew died – more than were lost by Fighter Com-

mand during the Battle of Britain – in a raid on Berlin. When the Battle of Berlin opened in August 1943, a new tactic was used. A Master Bomber would circle the target, guiding the planes. Selected for this dangerous task was W/C Johnny Fauquier, a Canadian. He later dropped in rank from Air Commodore to Group Captain to continue flying, and led the RCAF's own Pathfinders.

Canada went to war with 3100 members in its air force and 210 planes, only 36 of which were fit for combat, in eight squadrons. By the end of the conflict, 232,500 men and 17,000 women had served in the RCAF, which by then had 48 squadrons. A total of 17,100 died as Canadian airmen who had served in a wide range of operations in many theatres of war.

Below: *Two RCAF Hurricane pilots scramble from York, England, during 1941.*

Right: *Workers at an aircraft factory at Malton, Ontario, put the finishing touches to a Lysander. These planes flew secret agents and arms to France.*

Canadians made up a quarter of 617 Squadron, the RAF's famous 'Dam Busters,' which defended the besieged island of Malta. Late in 1941, Blenheims of Canada's 404 Squadron of Coastal Command covered a commando raid on Vaasgo, Norway. In July in the following year, seven Canadian Kittyhawks of 111 Squadron left Elmendorf air base in Alaska for Umnak, the advanced American base in the Aleutians, after the Japanese landed on Kiska and Attu. Four flew into mountainsides, and one wandered out to sea. Canadian crews scoured the seas for signs of U-boats, and destroyed 27 of them. F/Lt. D. F. Raynes, piloting a Digby of Eastern Air Command, sank the U-520 on 30 October 1942, the first of six submarines to fall to this group. Two nights after D-Day, F/O K. O. Moore, flying a Liberator, located and sank two U-boats in less than half an hour off the coast of France.

Canadians flew spares for Hurricane planes to Russia, and fighters supported troops at the Sangro River, Cassino and Anzio in Italy. They also towed gliders carrying troops who attempted to seize the bridge at Arnhem on 17 September 1944.

S/L Leonard J. Birchall became known as the 'saviour of Ceylon.' After patrolling the waters off Norway, Birchall was piloting a Catalina of 413 Squadron over the Indian Ocean on 4 April 1942, when his crew spotted a dot on the horizon. Flying closer, they identified a large Japanese fleet on its way to attack Colombo, the British fleet base on Ceylon (now Sri Lanka). Birchall radioed the position, course and speed of the fleet and the British repulsed the attack. A Japanese plane shot down the Catalina, and two crew members died in strafing. Six others survived, and Birchall received the Distinguished Flying Cross and an O.B.E. for his conduct in a Japanese prisoner-of-war camp.

Canadian Dakotas dropped supplies to troops pushing the Japanese out of Burma in January 1945. Two of the unarmed transport fell to Japanese fighters. As the war in the Far East ended, Canadian planes flew rice to starving people in northern Burma.

The European air war can be divided into three phases: the defence of Britain by fighters, the bomber offensive over Germany, and then, as plans came to fruition for the invasion of Europe, a period of tactical bombing in support of troops fighting on land.

As a condition for initiating the British Commonwealth Air Training Plan, the Canadian government insisted that RCAF squadrons be formed overseas. When the war started, about 1000 Canadians were either in the Royal Air Force or training as aircrew. Some of these 'CAN/RAF' men joined 242 (Canadian) Squadron, RAF, formed on 30 October 1939, at Church Fenton, Yorkshire. On 1 November, S/L Fowler Gobeil, a career RCAF officer, assumed command, with P/O Peter MacDonald as adjutant. Born in Halifax, MacDonald had gone overseas in 1915 with the Canadian Expeditionary Force, been wounded and commissioned. After the war he had stayed in England,

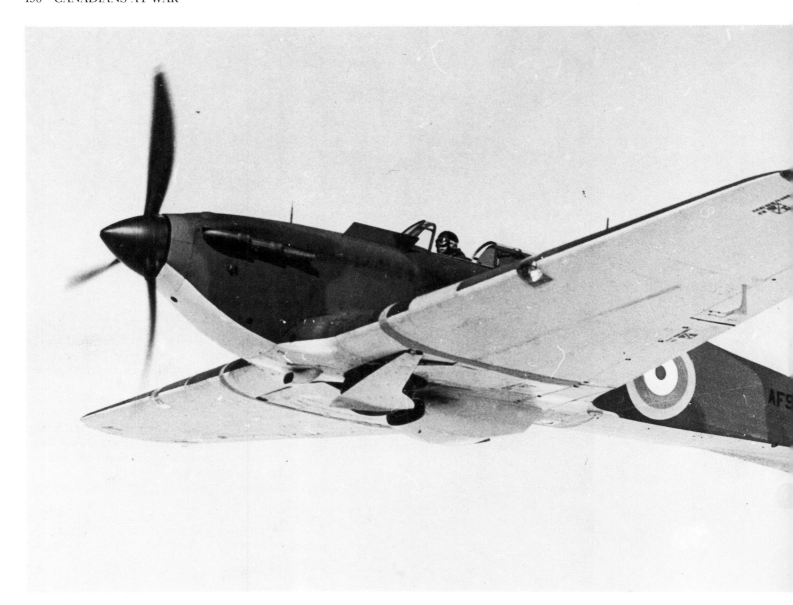

Above: *One of the Hurricane fighters built at Fort William, Ontario (now Thunder Bay). The plant turned out 15 Hurricane fighters a week for Britain in 1941.*

Left: *This Stranraer of the RCAF patrolled off Canada's east coast early in the war, searching for submarines.*

qualified as a lawyer, and been elected to Parliament for the Isle of Wight in 1924. He retained his seat while serving with the RAF. Most of the Canadians in 242 had secured their pilot's licenses at their own expense in Canada. They included a bank clerk, a bandleader, a gold miner, a medical student, a dairyman, and a civil engineer. The ground crew came mainly from Britain. Flying Hurricanes, the squadron patrolled the skies of France and Belgium as the British troops retreated toward Dunkirk. After the evacuation of these soldiers from the beaches, 242 Squadron flew into a field near Nantes as the Canadian 1st Brigade advanced into France. By this time, the pilots had shot down 30 enemy planes, and had seven of their number killed and two wounded. In France they had to fuel, arm, service and guard their own planes. On 18 June, the squadron flew one last sortie over France. Then they evacuated the airfield, feeling anger rather than relief as they soared through empty skies over a peaceful land.

On 24 June, S/L Douglas Bader took command of 242. He had had both legs amputated after an accident in 1931, but persuaded the RAF to take him back, and had a rare combination of courage, charm, rudeness and humanity.

In the same month, Canada's No. 1 Squadron arrived at Middle Wallop, flying stubby-winged Hurricanes that had to be modified before they could go into combat. S/L E. A. McNab shot down a German Dornier on 15 August to claim the RCAF's first victory. Eleven days later he went after German bombers, which shot him down with two of his com-

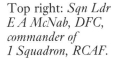

Top right: *Sqn Ldr E A McNab, DFC, commander of 1 Squadron, RCAF.*

Right: *The Operations Room of a Fighter Command base during the Battle of Britain.*

panions. McNab crash-landed as did one other pilot, but F/O R. L. Edwards became the RCAF's first death in aerial combat.

The Battle of Britain lasted from 10 July to 31 October 1940, but the Germans failed in their aim of knocking the British air force out of the sky as a prelude to an invasion of England. On 24 August, in the confusion of battle, McNab and his pilots shot down three British Blenheims near Portsmouth. A week later, while patrolling over Dover, Messerschmitts came out of the sun and attacked the squadron. Three pilots bailed out as their planes disintegrated under the Germans' guns. In the afternoon, the Canadians shot down a Bf 109 and damaged one more, with another pilot successfully knocking down a Dornier.

S/L Bader restored the shattered morale of 242 Squadron and led them on the offensive, escorting bombers over France, shooting up enemy ships in the English Channel, and strafing enemy troop concentrations in sudden attacks known as 'rhubarbs.' On 12 January 1941, F/O 'Willie' McKnight, an

original squadron member with 16 enemy aircraft to his credit, was killed in action. On 3 April of that year, F/L Tamblyn, protecting a convoy east of Felixstowe, crashed into the sea after attacking a Dornier. He died of exposure and cold, his watch stopped at 9 a.m. just two days after receiving the DFC at Buckingham Palace.

By June 1941, only three Canadian pilots remained in 242. Then, Sgt. Casgrain, flying back from attacking shipping, died when another Canadian pilot mistook him for a German and fired a two-second burst at his Hurricane. Posted to Sumatra in 1942, the squadron fought without hope against the Japanese invaders and ceased to exist when the island fell.

In all, 42 Canadians served with 242, accounting for 47 of the 105-and-a-half enemy aircraft credited to the squadron, and losing 24 of their fellows either killed or made prisoners of war. On 10 April 1942, a new 242 Squadron came into being. No longer designated 'Canadian,' it scored its first probable with the guns of Flt. Sgt. John Portz of the RCAF who

hailed from Weyburn, Saskatchewan.

Many RCAF messes and ready rooms contained a poster that stated, 'There are old pilots, and bold pilots; there are no old, bold pilots.' Survival on operations for both fighter and bomber pilots depended on recognition that every person fought as a member of a team, inside the aircraft and in the formations. The poet W. H. Auden called fighter pilots 'the closest modern equivalent to the Homeric hero.' But every pilot fought under a leader who gave the orders. They looked out for enemy aircraft, and warned their companions of attacks, covering them in combat.

The highest-scoring British and Commonwealth ace during the Second World War prided himself on being a loner. Flying became a passion with 'Buzz' Beurling, also nicknamed 'Screwball.' He flew first at the age of nine, and soloed at 16. When the RCAF rejected him because he had not completed high school, Beurling crossed the Atlantic and enlisted in the RAF. Over Calais on 3 May 1942, Beurling 'bagged' a Hun, peeling off from the flight to attack the leader of a squadron of Focke-Wulfs. Beurling

flew back alone to his base. Here he found his fellow pilots had already landed, and were complaining about him. His commanding officer noted that he had left a companion's tail uncovered and told him, 'That's not done, old man.' And so Beurling stayed on the ground while other pilots went on sweeps, seeking out enemy planes.

Beurling identified three factors in the 'fighter pilot's business:' flying, shooting, and physical fitness, which included excellent eyesight. He had that sixth sense so vital to a pilot – an uncanny ability to recognize when an enemy plane presented the best target.

Posted to Malta, Beurling came into his own with 249 Squadron. The island of Malta lay athwart the German supply lines to North Africa, where General Rommel had pushed the British army back to within 100 kilometres of Alexandria. The German Air Force (the Luftwaffe) sought to destroy the island. Squadrons of fighters, bombers, and torpedo planes fought them off and attacked German ships trying to bring supplies to Rommel's Afrika Corps. Flying from Takali airfield, George Beurling downed 27 German and Italian aircraft, damaged eight others, and scored three probables in the summer of 1942. Failing to look behind him when he went into an attack on 14 October, Beurling's luck ran out. Wounded and shot down over the sea, he was rescued and left Malta on 1 November. An officer by then, Beurling had a cast on his leg – and a Distinguished Service Order alongside a DFC as well as a Distinguished Flying Medal and Bar. He returned to Canada a hero, and in 1943 collaborated with Leslie Roberts on his autobiography *Malta Spitfire*. In an introduction, Billy Bishop saluted 'Canada's young falcon of Malta.'

Promoted to flight lieutenant in the RCAF, Beurling added three more enemy planes to his score for a total of 31-and-a-half. But he resented service discipline, and was reprimanded for low flying in a Tiger Moth. He left the RCAF in October 1944.

Wally McLeod, another ace, also received blasts from his commanding officer for failing to fly in for-

mation and ignoring instructions. Born in Regina, Saskatchewan, McLeod earned a living before the war by showing movies in church and school halls out west, joining up as an AC2 on 2 September 1940. Like Beurling, he found his war in Malta, earning a DSO, DFC and Bar. He claimed that his first victim, an Italian Macchi, went into the sea from sheer fright. Near Sicily, McLeod shot down a German Bf 109. The pilot fell clear, his parachute opened, and he drifted down to the sea. McLeod circled him, and the downed flier waved to him. To show that he had no hard feelings, McLeod dropped a dinghy to his enemy. But the German did not climb into it – he had a cannon shell wound in his chest, and died in the rescue launch.

Like Beurling, McLeod conserved ammunition in combat by precise shooting, knocking down two planes with 13 shells from each of his two cannon on 23 June 1944. At this time he was flying Spitfires over France. On 30 July, McLeod made his twenty-first kill to become the top-scoring RCAF ace. Patrolling beyond the Rhine on 27 September, McLeod failed to turn in time as a Bf 109 came at him in a fast dive. His remains, still in his Spitfire, were found by advancing Canadian troops.

Left: *Sqn Ldr 'Wally' McLeod, top-scoring RCAF pilot, commanded 443 Squadron in 1944, and was killed in September of that year.*

Below: *Spitfires of No. 92 Squadron scramble from Manston airfield, 1941. The two nearer aircraft are cannon-armed Mk Ibs.*

Right: *These Tiger Moths were used to train pilots in the RCAF.*

Canadian airmen won two Victoria Crosses during the war for acts of supreme courage. On the night of 12 June 1944, a Lancaster bomber set out to attack the railyards at Cambrai. P/O Andy Mynarski, a turret gunner, found a four-leaf clover just before takeoff and gave it to his friend Pat Brophy, the rear gunner. They were on their 13th mission. As the bomber crossed the French coast, searchlights 'coned' it, catching it in their beams so that anti-aircraft guns could hit it and nightfighters could find it. As the Lancaster neared its target, a Ju 88 roared toward it, its guns knocking out two engines and setting the plane on fire. Inside the doomed plane, red lights flashed, signalling the crew to bail out. Pat Brophy tried to rotate his turret to bail out, and found it jammed. Mynarski saw the plight of his friend, and crawled down through the blazing plane to free him. On fire, he failed to move the turret, and Brophy urged him to save himself. Mynarski went out of the escape hatch, pausing only to salute his friend. The Lancaster dove into the earth and exploded. Brophy, thrown from his turret, survived the crash. Mynarski landed alive, but died from his burns.

F/L David Hornell piloted a Catalina out of Wick in northern Scotland, endlessly searching for enemy submarines in the seas between Iceland and Britain. On 24 June 1944, a crew member spotted a U-boat on the surface north of the Faroes. In the plane and on the submarine the crews sprang to action stations, for by now the Germans had decided to fight it out on the surface with attacking aircraft rather than waiting to be depth-charged. As the Catalina swooped down, 37-mm and 20-mm guns on the U-boat opened up, setting it ablaze. Hornell bore in, landing his depth charges right on the submarine.

Then his plane crashed into the sea. The crew clung to a dinghy in heavy seas until rescuers arrived 24 hours later. By that time, two men had died. And for David Hornell, help also came too late.

By the end of 1941, the RCAF had formed four bomber squadrons. But at the beginning of the next year they had only 71 aircraft, 27 of them classified 'non-operational.' The Canadians flew Hampdens and Wellingtons, and throughout the war were usually the last to receive the most modern bombers and the most sophisticated equipment. Operating from airfields in Yorkshire, the crews had the longest distance to fly to targets in Europe and back. Many Canadians chose to serve in the RAF. In fact, Sir Arthur 'Bomber' Harris – also known as 'Butcher' Harris – who commanded the bombers, wrote twice to the Air Ministry, complaining about the increase in 'Foreign and Dominion' elements in the RAF and his own command. By 1943 he was expressing concern that already half of the aircrew in his command were 'non-UK identity.' In the case of Canadians, Harris may have been upset by their attitudes toward rank and class. Andy Mynarski and Pat Brophy shared the same perils in the sky as aerial gunners, but when they first became friends, Mynarski was a noncommissioned officer and Brophy an officer. On Canadian stations, sergeants and officers deserted their messes and retired to the local pub to talk and drink together. The Canadians pressed for commissions for all aircrew, and won their case in early 1944. A British historian stated that the Canadians had 'both logic and humanity' on their side. Their approach was more suited to a large, modern, technical service than that of the RAF, where only those with 'officer-like qualities' would receive commissions.

Left: *Lancaster ED905 takes off on its 100th mission, 4 November 1944.*

Above: *F/Lt Cybulski (right) and his radar operator L H A Cadbrook with their Mosquito, after an encounter with a Dornier 217 which they shot down on 26 September 1943.*

Right: *Hugh Godefroy of 401 Squadron won the DFC in 1943, and led 127 Wing in 1944, adding a DSO and a Bar to his DFC.*

Bomber Harris believed that Germany could be defeated by bombing its cities – and particularly Berlin – into dust and breaking the morale of the people. He began his talk at one Canadian station by saying that, 'More than half of you won't be here in a few weeks.' Only one crew out of three survived 30 missions to complete a tour of 'ops.'

Canadian fliers who survived and wrote their memoirs recalled every detail of the preparation for bombing missions. Crews assembled in the Operations Room, where a map showed a red ribbon leading from their base to the target. The Commanding Officer spoke, identifying the target, telling of the bomb loads, special tactics, and the importance of the mission. The intelligence office shared his 'gen' – the information on the hazards of the operation – and then came a briefing on the weather. Carrying their gear, the crews went out to their planes. Now began the worst moments – waiting for takeoff. All the fliers became superstitious. Some urinated on the tail wheel for luck, others carried small ivory elephants, good luck dolls, or stuffed toys. One man wore an old hockey sweater.

The men who wrote about their war in the air paid tribute to the ground crews who serviced, fuelled and armed the planes before they thundered off into the darkness. Each squadron had 20 crews, and one writer recalls that in the first month of 1944 his unit lost exactly that number of crews. Weather proved as treacherous an enemy as flak and fighters. The Bomber Command developed ways of outfoxing the fighters and the radar by dumping out 'window' – strips of aluminum foil that generated images.

The Germans attacked the bombers from underneath with fixed, upward firing guns. The British planes had no protection from this *schräge Musik*. The casualties on bombing raids over Germany resembled those of the infantry in attacks on the Western Front in the First World War. On 2-3 January 1944, 383 bombers set out for Berlin. Sixty turned back for various reasons, but the others pressed on. From that mission, 26 Lancasters failed to return, and 168 aircrew died. Another 31 became prisoners. On 20 January, the bombers went back to Berlin, and the loss on that night was 172 killed, 75 made prisoners of war, and ten others who evaded capture after being shot down. A week later the bombers set off again for the German capital. Again, 172 aircrew died when 33 Lancasters failed to return. Four men managed to evade capture, but 55 others became prisoners of war.

On the first sortie in the Battle of Berlin on 23 August 1943, a Ju 88 raked a Stirling, wounding the pilot. The bomb aimer, a Canadian sergeant, John Bailey, had almost completed his pilot training before being 'washed out.' He took over, piloted the plane home to its base, and received an immediate commission and the Conspicuous Gallantry Medal.

RCAF bombers had first gone into action when 68 planes joined the first 1000-bomber raid on Cologne in May 1942. On 1 January 1943, 11 Canadian squadrons came together to form the all-Canadian No. 6 Bomber Group. Between 5 March and 24 June 1943, the Group lost 100 planes. A year after its formation, Air Vice-Marshal C. M. 'Black Mike' McEwen took command, and the group

began to fly Canadian-made Lancasters with more effective navigation and bombing aides. The Lancasters proved to be much more effective bombers, able to carry heavier loads than the Halifaxes and Stirlings. These two aircraft also had significantly higher losses during missions. By the end of 1944, No. 6 Group had the lowest casualties of any in Bomber Command.

Murray Peden enlisted in the RCAF at 18. He passed through Initial Training School, Elementary Flying Training School, and Service Flying Training School in Canada. Then he went to England to complete his training at Advanced Flying Unit (on Oxfords) and Operational Training Unit (on Wellingtons). It was when Peden first saw the Wellingtons at Chipping Warden that he became 'sharply aware of the nearer presence of the God of War.' Part of his training involved investigating the place where a plane had crashed on a night exercise, killing all the crew, a mile or two from the station.

On 24 July 1943, Peden went on his first operation – a leaflet-dropping raid over Montargis, a town about 60 miles south of Paris. Before the crew left they received a treat – a fried egg and toast supper. All aircrew who served in Britain recall the sheer inedibility of British food and the heavy reliance on brussel sprouts as the mainstay of meals.

Tension mounted when the enemy coast appeared. Ahead of Peden's plane 'C Charlie' a flash lit the sky – one of the Wellingtons ('Wimpies') had been shot down. Peden could not land at Chipping Warden, as it was fogged in. The next airfield also lay wreathed in mist, and the controller suggested that Peden fly inland. Finally Peden saw a runway and landed safely. Of the three other Wellingtons in the

Below: A Battle of Britain Spitfire Mk II of No. 602 Squadron. Many Canadians flew in RAF fighter squadrons during the battle.

Right: The deadly beauty of a Handley-Page Halifax of 405 Squadron in flight. It replaced the Wellington and became the favourite of RCAF aircrew.

sortie, one had been shot down, one had crashed on landing and another had been heavily damaged when it came down on a runway on which obstacles had been placed. None of the crews had been lost, however. Back at the base, the crew revelled in real fried eggs, and the attention of members of the Women's Auxiliary Air Force who obviously recognized 'pukka operational types just back from a trip over enemy territory.' Through Peden's memoirs runs a strain of brash cheerfulness, tinged with fear and grief for the death of friends as the war grimly ground on.

In August, Peden 'converted' to Stirling bombers from the two-engined Wellingtons. The wheels of the Stirling stood as tall as a man, but the huge undercarriage proved to be a weak spot in the plane when buffeted by a cross wind, making the bomber hard to handle. On 22 August, Peden secured a certificate stating that he knew how to correct and prevent swinging of Stirling aircraft.

On 21 September 1943, Peden received his posting to 214 Squadron, and that evening he ate dinner in the mess at Stradishall wondering 'with a mixture of excitement and dread what a real target would be like.' On the following night he found out, while flying 'second dickey' (extra pilot) with an experienced crew. The Stirlings took off at sunset for Hanover. Peden saw a bomber stream smoke and then dive to earth. Another plane slid toward theirs, and Peden grabbed the controls and avoided a collision with it. He recalls the fear that gripped the crew as they flew toward the target. Because of a navigational error, the plane initially missed its target, and had to return to bomb it. Hanover's anti-aircraft batteries opened up on the solitary plane, but it survived the flak and headed for home. After landing, Peden watched a straggler arrive – and saw another pair of navigation lights approaching it. They belonged to a German fighter bomber which shot up the Stirling and then dropped butterfly bombs on the field.

Peden obviously had keen senses and excellent eyesight. He also flew with a friendly, skilled crew when he captained his own Stirling. Their first trip together involved 'Gardening' – dropping mines – and took only three hours and thirty-five minutes. The Canadian pilot flew in the days of the RAF's 'Maximum Effort,' the time when Bomber Harris concentrated his forces on targets in Germany and the Germans put their efforts into developing effective night fighter tactics and organizing flak batteries to protect their cities.

For a while Peden, given special training, dropped supplies to the Maquis fighting the Germans in France, an operation that required precision flying at low levels. He showed a great talent for this kind of work. His twelfth mission took Peden to Le Havre to lay mines at low level – and then came what the crews called No. 12A. The aircraft Peden flew turned out to be a lemon. The undercarriage failed to retract automatically and had to be cranked up manually. Then the H2S radar set's screen blew up, and they failed to find the field where they were to drop supplies to the Maquis.

Early in January 1944, Murray Peden received word of the death of his friend Rod Dunphy and other fliers he knew who had 'got the chop.' Death touched without distinction the experienced ones and the newcomers, skilled crews and merely adequate ones, the optimists and the pessimists.

The survivors pressed on. Those who refused to fly were branded L.M.F. ('Lack of Moral Fiber'), reduced to AC2, the lowest rank in the air force, and posted away.

Murray Peden, one of the few Canadian pilots to man Flying Fortresses, bombed targets in France before the invasion of Europe, and took off in 'F Fox' for a target in the Ruhr known as 'Happy Valley' on 21 June. Behind him a Lancaster dove away, and an Me 410 opened fire on Peden's plane. The starboard inner engine burst into flames, and the bomber began to lose height. Another night fighter, drawn by the fire, attacked F Fox. Dodging and weaving, Peden proved the plane to be as clever as its official designation, and flew the shattered machine back to base. As F Fox touched down, Peden discovered that his right tire had been shot to pulp, and as he fought the machine to the ground it hit a Lancaster. Peden learned later that it carried a 5000-kilo bomb; its crew died two weeks later on its last op.

On 29 August, Peden bombed Stettin and slumped wearily into his seat after piloting the Fortress for eight hours and fifty minutes. On 8 September, he took his log book to the office of his squadron commander who endorsed his First Tour. With his crew, Peden had survived his tour as a heavy bomber pilot.

Walter Thompson arrived to train in Yorkton, Saskatchewan, on 8 November 1942, when it appeared that Britain might lose the war. The trainees ate under paintings of Bishop, Collishaw, McLaren and Barker – aces of the First World War – on the walls of the mess. On 9 March 1943, Thompson prepared to 'smite the Hun' as the pilot of a Pathfinder with W/C Guy Gibson of 106 Squadron. He would later claim that he navigated his way around Germany by the flak and the searchlights.

One account tells of W/C R.J. Lane, codenamed Redskin, serving as Master Bomber in a plane that stayed over Berlin for 20 minutes, providing directions to the other bombers as they sought their targets. He also gave encouragement in an excited voice, calling, 'Those bastards wanted a war; now show them what war is like.' Other messages are not printable, the source notes.

Thompson saw pilots arrive at the squadron looking like scared rabbits. They quickly disappeared. To Thompson, fear was the killer. He felt stimulated on missions, becoming more afraid of cowardice than of death. The pilot felt the joy of battle when he went on missions to bomb missile sites from which the Germans launched V-1 rockets to England. That feeling vanished when he realized that, because of the inability of Pathfinders to mark targets accurately, the bombs were simply killing people rather than hitting industrial plants. His crew became self-

Top right: A Mosquito of 418 Squadron. Built in Canada of wood, these fast, light planes served with Fighter Command and the Tactical Air Force.

Right: W/C 'Buck' McNair won the DSO and DFC and two Bars for shooting down 16 enemy planes.

Far right: Canada's leading night fighter ace, W/C 'Moose' Fumerton, DFC, destroyed 13 enemy planes in the air – and one on the ground.

sufficient, tight-lipped, worn down by the stress of combat. On his last trip, Thompson asked God for courage to carry out the operation with precision and courage; he had never prayed before in his life. As he headed for Canada, the pilot recognized that, for all its perils, he had lived his finest hour in Britain.

Doug Harvey, as a sergeant pilot, went to Gelsenkirchen in 'Happy Valley' on his first mission as an observer. He shut down one engine as the Halifax passed through the belt of searchlights and anti-aircraft guns on the French coast. On the return from the target, the bomber twisted, turned and corkscrewed to avoid the bullets of a night fighter. Tracer shells knocked out another engine, and the Halifax began to sink lower. Harvey suggested to the pilot that they try to restart the engine they had shut down on the way to the target. It worked well enough to bring them back to their base.

Harvey's last mission, on 30 March 1944, took him to Nuremburg with 800 other aircraft. In that raid 97 bombers went down. Harvey recalls the aromas of oil, grease, and gasoline as he climbed into his plane, and the smell of fear as he saw night fighters attacking the bombers. Lancasters exploded, while fire flickered along the wings and fuselages of others. Accounts of raids tell of planes dropping their bombs on others below them. On one occasion, a Canadian airman saw six planes explode as they opened their bomb doors. This action triggered the bombs before they left the plane, and in this case a bomb must have gone off prematurely.

Doug Harvey brought his crew and plane back safely from Nuremburg after seven-and-a-half hours in the air. Then he heard the magic words — 'You're screened' – and realized that he would not have to fly any more missions.

Dave McIntosh summed up his sentiments in the title of his book *Terror in the Starboard Seat*. He flew 41 missions in a Mosquito. A thousand of these very fast twin-engined planes were produced in Canada and engaged in what McIntosh called 'murder by night.' He added that the plane killed by day, too, with 2000-kilo bombs, cannon, machine guns, and even an anti-tank gun. McIntosh joined the RCAF in 1942 after being rejected by the army and the navy. He trained as a navigator, and recalls a pep talk given by 'Buzz' Beurling to inspire the airmen. Beurling spoke of blowing the head off the pilot of a white Italian plane over Malta – then threw back his head and laughed.

McIntosh served with 418 Squadron in England, in a Mosquito piloted by Sid Seid. They chased and shot down V-1 rockets and patrolled German airfields at night on the watch for planes landing and taking off. McIntosh writes vividly of his fear as the plane swept over Europe, and compared flak to orange, yellow and red tennis balls that appeared to come right through the nose of the Mosquito.

J. K. Chapman provides few details of his time in the air, describing himself as a 'survivor' rather than a hero. Inspired by pulp magazines like *War Aces* and *Flying Aces*, he enlisted in the RCAF in November 1940. Trained as a navigator, Chapman served in torpedo- and bomb-carrying Hampdens of 415 Squadron, Coastal Command. In June and July 1942, it lost six crews. Only one man survived, spending 14 days in a dinghy in the North Sea and having his legs amputated after rescue. Chapman, like other survivors, tells of the noisy parties and wild drinking in the messes, describing them as wakes for dead friends. Chapman married before going overseas, and returned to Canada after a year on operations. He had left the country a boy, and returned a man – gray-haired, 15 kilos under-weight, fingers stained with nicotine, and suffering from insomnia. But he cherished the knowledge and experience he had gained in his terrifying coming of age, and remembered with affection the friends he made.

Richard Rohmer, flying a Mustang on a reconnaissance mission on 24 April 1944, had 'a bit of a twitch' as he headed for Dieppe. The 20-year old Flying Officer viewed himself as an invincible fighter pilot with a gung-ho attitude. He followed the 12th Spitfire attacking shipping in Dieppe harbour, and suddenly found himself the focus of all the flak guns in the area. He survived the ordeal, took photographs, and returned to base. Only one photograph came out, and it showed nothing of significance. On 13 May, Rohmer successfully photographed 'Noball' sites near St. Omer that had been bombed. No one told him what the sites were – and he did not ask. They contained ramps for launching the V-1 rockets against England.

After D-Day, Rohmer's plane ran into flak that holed it 13 times as he took shots of motor transport near Caen on 13 July. Then the pilot became the eyes of the Canadian and British troops, watching enemy movements, and calling in rocket-firing Typhoons and bomb-carrying Spitfires as he spotted targets. Forbidden to attack ground targets, Rohmer watched in frustration as columns of German armour poured through the Falaise Gap during their retreat from Normandy in August 1944.

S/L Norman Fowlow, a Newfoundlander, had served in Malta, and been shot down on his second sortie. Before D-Day he flew sweeps over France, using his Spitfire as a dive bomber. On 19 May 1944, Fowlow attacked a railway crossing at Hazebrouck, France, as part of the 'softening-up' process before the invasion. Flak hit the plane, exploding the 200-kilo bomb slung below it and the Spitfire disintegrated 2000 meters above the ground.

Robert Collins, a Saskatchewan farm boy, served with No. 6 Bomber Group's ground crew. He compared his first encounter with a Lancaster to a mouse surveying an elephant. Collins learned air force jargon, endured dried eggs, powdered milk and mutton in the mess, bartered cigarettes for eggs with the local farmers, and discovered the joys of English pubs. After the war in Europe ended, Collins fell into a state of limbo before joining the British Air Force of Occupation. He served at a former Luftwaffe base near Hamburg, now renamed RCAF 126 Wing, servicing Spitfires whose very name stirred his imagination.

Collins' war ended in March 1946, when the Wing

left Germany. Demobilized in July, he left the RCAF with three medals and a gratuity of $421.57. Under an ex-serviceman's program, Collins received free tuition and $60 a month for expenses while he studied at university. The war turned Collins from a shy prairie boy into a confident man, grateful for the courage and endurance of those who fought at the sharp end of war.

Murray Peden caught the very essence of what the time in combat meant to him – and to every other Canadian who flew constantly into danger, night after night, day after day:

> *I look back on that period with 214 Squadron as a time both wonderful and terrible. It was wonderful in the sense that never is fragile life so precious and rewarding as when we cannot count on savouring it for more than another day, one more Battle Order. Our joys were thus intense. It was a terrible time precisely because of that reverse side of the coin: the frequent and heartbreaking loss of friends, the repressed fear of having to fly yet again through bursting flak, prowling night fighters, and the blinding glare of searchlights. But to have survived these, and passed the test of self-control they imposed, is to have fallen heir to an entirely new perspective for the rest of one's life, a marvellous measuring rod that shrinks subsequent trials. And sometimes, secretly, a man cannot help feeling a little proud that he paid the high price of admission, and can walk unchallenged in the company of a small group of similarly-tested brothers. In His own way, God favoured us richly.*

The air war transformed the country as well as individuals. The British Commonwealth Air Training Plan trained 131,553 aircrew, more than 55 percent of them Canadian, at a cost of $1.6 billion. The Second World War opened up the Canadian North as airfields built in the Eastern Arctic served to ferry planes to Europe. In Western Canada the Alaska Highway pushed up through northern British Columbia and the Yukon Territory to Fairbanks, flanked by a string of airfields. Canada's experiences in the air and in ground support during the Second World War showed how skilled and courageous men, with good leadership and modern technology, could endure and play a vital role in securing victory against great odds.

AT SEA

Looking back at the RCN's contribution to the Second
World War, one cannot but conclude that the impossible
was achieved but the miracles remained elusive.
MARC MILNER, *North Atlantic Run* (1985)

When Newfoundlander Jack Gillingham learned of the outbreak of war, he took his discharge book from the Merchant Navy in which he had served for 17 years, and headed for the naval recruiting station. An officer looked at the book and said, 'You're in. You're the kind we need!' A medical examination discovered a large pleurisy scar on one of Gillingham's lungs. But three days later, and without any training, he was on a ship patrolling the coast. The defence of Canada's west coast depended on the Fishermen's Reserve, which manned 15 ships of the fishing fleet.

The Royal Canadian Navy (RCN) entered the war with six modern destroyers, five small minesweepers and two training vessels, one a sailing ship. Directed by ten men in three offices in Ottawa, the RCN had only 145 officers and 1674 men. The professionals saw the navy's role as protecting Canada's coasts. Rear-Admiral Percy Nelles, Chief of the Naval Staff, ignored the lessons of the First World War, claiming that 'if international law is complied with, submarine attack should not prove serious.'

The RCN sent its six destroyers to protect England at the start of the war. During the Dunkirk

Left: *U-210 under attack by HMCS* Assiniboine, *which rammed and sank her on 6 August 1942.*

Above: *A convoy steams across the perilous North Atlantic to Britain in March 1941.*

evacuation in June 1940, HMCS *Fraser*, sliced in two by a British cruiser, sank with the loss of 40 men.

With beleaguered Britain relying on supplies from the United States and Canada, the Battle of the Atlantic began. Germany had 26 U-boats when war began. They sank 217 merchant ships displacing just over 1.1 million tons between July and October 1940. The period between January and June 1941 became known as *die Glückliche Zeit* – 'the Happy Time' – by U-boat crews. They sank 2.9 million tons of Allied shipping with little opposition, and in 1942 another six million tons went to the bottom of the Atlantic. In an attack on Convoy SC-107 in August, 16 U-boats sank 15 out of 42 ships. Directed by Admiral Karl Doenitz, a former submariner, U-boat commanders pressed home attacks, co-operating in wolf packs and using information transmitted from their bases on the destinations and makeup of Allied convoys.

Canada's war at sea, directed by the 'pusser' (proper) navy, was fought by the 'meadow-green men,' volunteers who joined the Royal Canadian Naval Volunteer Service (RCNVR). Together with a handful of merchant seaman commissioned into the Royal Canadian Naval Reserve (RCNR), these amateurs from field, factory and office manned escort vessels, corvettes, minesweepers, Fairmile launches, motor torpedo boats, and landing craft. As one corvette captain put it, 'We had two enemies: the U-boats and the weather. I often wondered which was the worst.'

Left: *Merchant Navy survivors of U-boat attacks land from SS Bury in Halifax on 19 May 1942.*

Right: *Every Canadian sailor faced two enemies – the Germans and the North Atlantic weather. This photo shows ice build-up on HMCS Lunenburg in Halifax Harbour, January 1942.*

Below: *HMCS* Andrée Dupré, *on which Hal Lawrence started his wartime service in Halifax.*

Some Canadians served with the Royal Navy. In late October 1940, Warren Stevens of the RCNR shipped out of Halifax on the armed merchant cruiser *Jervis Bay*. On 8 November, the German battleship *Admiral Scheer* attacked the convoy she was protecting. Hit and on fire, the *Jervis Bay* headed straight for the enemy, her six-inch guns no match for the battleship's 11-inch batteries. Mortally wounded, Captain Fogarty Fegen fought back with only one gun in action, dropping smoke bombs to conceal the ships in the convoy and give them time to escape. Stevens saw five ships go up in flames, then put on a cork lifejacket and went over the side of the doomed merchant cruiser. Pulled from the waters of the North Atlantic with legs that felt like dead meat, Stevens was one of seven Canadian sailors to survive. Another 19 went down with the 200 killed in the gallant fight of the *Jervis Bay*.

Hitler, fearing the loss of his big ships, kept them in port, and Germany relied on its submarines to win the war at sea. Badly trained, poorly equipped, and lacking co-ordination, Canada's seamen took over increasing responsibility for protecting the convoys. The little ships sailed on the Triangle Run between New York, Halifax and Saint John's and from 'Slackers' (Halifax) and Sydney to 'Derry (Londonderry in Northern Ireland).

The career of one naval officer shows the calibre

of Canada's new seamen. Hal Lawrence joined the navy as an RCNVR midshipman on 8 September 1939, enthralled with the idea of serving on big battlecruisers. He began his service in a grey, grubby tug, the *Andrée Dupré* in Halifax Harbour, and soon learned the limits of the courses he had taken ashore. The tug had neither guns nor torpedoes. Since it stayed in harbour, navigation presented no problems. And the signals system simply involved exchanging messages with flashing lamps. Lawrence moved to the HMS *Alaunia*, an armed merchant cruiser, on convoy duty. By September 1941, he was on the corvette HMCS *Moose Jaw* off Greenland awaiting a U-boat attack. Like other corvettes, Lawrence's ship was named after a Canadian city. Hastily-built for convoy duty, corvettes had been designed like whalers on the premise that a vessel that could chase a huge sea mammal should also be able to find and sink a submarine. Corvettes earned the love and hatred of many Canadian sailors, and Canada built more than 130 of them. A solitary four-inch gun sat on the bow of the stubby, 205-foot-long craft, and it was said that these vessels rolled on wet grass. Crewed by 42 officers and men, corvettes continued to be refitted and modified throughout the war, and each developed its own individuality.

In 1943, a twin-screwed version, the frigate, joined the RCN. The corvette's crew, jammed into a small forecastle where they slung their hammocks and also ate, had to suffer many miseries as the ship escorted the vital Atlantic convoys. During the long passages the bread grew moldier and the rats bolder. Stomach-sick sailors lay inert on lockers, waiting to be pushed out on to their next watch. Sleep had to be snatched whenever possible, and water sloshed around the deck, soaking everything. The small ships dipped and rose in the mountainous seas of the North Atlantic and slid through fog that settled around them like a shroud. Ice building up on exposed surfaces had to be chipped off or it could have capsized the vessel. An officer recalls a radar rating sent as after look-out in a storm. The savage seas bent the ship's plates, flattened the railing around a gun platform, and tore away a large raft. The lookout, knocked senseless by the water that swept over the ship's stern, simply vanished. He was only 19 years old.

The corvettes ploughed through the debris of torpedoed ships, seeking survivors, often unable to distinguish the living from the dead. On 19 September 1941, Canada lost its first corvette, HMCS *Levis*, when a torpedo ripped into her port bow. Broken-backed, the corvette stayed afloat for five hours before sinking with the loss of 17 of her crew.

After America entered the war, Canada sent six corvettes to the Caribbean to protect ships there. On

27 August 1942, Hal Lawrence, aboard HMCS *Oakville*, saw the black snout of U-94 rise out of the water south of Haiti. His captain tried to ram the submarine, but missed. Then the four-inch gun hit the conning tower as sailors used Lewis guns to kill the Germans trying to man the submarine's 88-mm deck piece. The Canadians threw Coke bottles as their ship closed with the U-boat. Lawrence led a boarding party, and jumped onto the deck of the submarine, his shorts sliding to his ankles as he advanced on the conning tower with another sailor. Ordering the crew on deck, Lawrence went below, scrambling out of the U-94 as she began to sink. Rescued by an American ship, Lawrence used naval language to convince its crew that he was a Canadian officer, not a German submariner. For his bravery he received the Distinguished Service Cross. Lawrence was also the *Oakville*'s only casualty in the action – he cut his elbow on a broken Coke bottle as he wiggled down the U-94's hatch.

Lawrence joined HMCS *Sioux*, a destroyer, and served on the run to Murmansk in Russia. With 50 other Canadian destroyers, frigates, corvettes and minesweepers, the *Sioux* protected the Allied invasion fleet on D-Day, 6 June 1944, and shelled enemy positions in France. In February 1945, *Sioux* again headed up the coast of Norway and came under attack by German planes as her crew closed up at

Top left: *The most uncomfortable, and valuable, warships that Canada produced – corvettes.*

Left: *Ratings muster on the starboard side of the destroyer HMCS* Assiniboine.

Above: *Depth charges leaving HMCS* Pictou, *March 1942.*

Cabot Strait. The corvette HMCS *Grandmere* attacked the submarine with depth charges, but she escaped by hiding under the passengers and crew struggling in the icy waters. Only 101 people survived; the 136 dead included 14 children and Agnes Wilkie, an RCNVR nursing sister. Her friend Margaret Brooke tried to sustain her but she slipped away. Brooke received the Order of the British Empire for her courage.

The Canadians who served on the little ships showed stamina and bravery as they battled the enemy and the seas. When the first corvettes sailed down the St. Lawrence, they carried wooden poles instead of four-inch guns. And the government had to appeal to the public for binoculars for the sailors manning the ships. Much of the Battle of the Atlantic was fought in darkness and heavy seas that made locating a U-boat, let alone destroying it, almost impossible. The only device for finding the submarines, asdic (Allied Submarine Detection Investigation Committee, also called sonar) pinged continually as the ships searched the ocean. But many submarines operated on the surface, their low silhouettes almost impossible to locate until they opened fire on ships with their deck guns. Planes flying from eastern Canada and Iceland could locate U-boats on the surface, but a large portion of the North Atlantic south of Greenland, known as 'the black pit,' could not be covered from the air.

The first submarine to be sunk by a Canadian ship, the U-501, formed part of a wolf pack that struck convoy SC-42 on 9-10 September 1941. The corvettes *Chambly* and *Moose Jaw* used depth charges, gunfire and ramming to sink her. *Chambly* put a boarding party on her, but U-501 sank, taking Stoker William Brown and 11 of her crew with her. Convoy SC-42 lost 15 merchant ships out of 64.

On 6 August 1942, HMCS *Assiniboine*, a destroyer captained by Lt. Cdr. John Stubbs, RCN, fought the U-210 in a fog bank. The submarine came in so close that the destroyer could not depress its main armament to fire at it, and Stubbs decided to ram. The submarine's guns riddled the destroyer's bridge and started a fire amidships. In the wheelhouse, Chief Petty Officer Max Bernays stayed at his post, carrying out orders while the flames roared outside the windows.

German submarines, built so strongly that they often survived attacks by depth charges, often limped back to base even when convoy escorts thought they had killed them. On one occasion, proof of success came in grisly fashion when a crewman on a corvette noticed what seagulls were picking up from the surface of the sea. A ship's boat retrieved the shattered remains of submariners.

A lack of co-operation between senior navy and air force officers made co-ordination of convoy protection difficult. To ensure supplies came through to Britain for the planned invasion of Europe, the Allies provided resources to their navies as the admirals and air marshals realized they had a common enemy – not just each other. Liberator bombers ranged over the ocean, direction-finding systems homed in on

action stations. After more convoy duty in those dark, icy, desperate seas, Lawrence's time in action ended. He would later write about it in the appropriately-titled memoir, *A Bloody War*.

American ships refused to use the convoy system. The U-boats had another happy time in 1942, sinking ships within sight of the cities on the eastern American seaboard. They also sailed up the St. Lawrence, sinking 23 ships with the loss of 700 lives in the Gulf and surrounding seas. A U-boat set up an automatic weather station in northern Labrador. In the summer of 1942, Lt. Cdr. Paul Hartwig in U-517 attacked a convoy bound for Greenland from Sydney, sinking the transport *Chatham*. Patrolling off Anticosti Island, he sank the *Donald Stewart*. Joined by U-165, Hartwig survived an air attack in which a bomb fell on the submarine, but failed to explode. He sank another ship in a Quebec-Sydney convoy, and slipped away as a corvette attacked. Another ship guarding the convoy, the armed yacht *Raccoon*, exploded, probably torpedoed by U-165. No trace of her, save for the body of one of her crew, was ever found. Off Gaspé, Hartwig sank the corvette HMCS *Charlottetown*, then fired his last four torpedoes at a convoy – and missed. Then he headed for home through Cabot Strait.

On 14 October 1942, the U-69 torpedoed and sank the Newfoundland car ferry *Caribou* in the

U-boat radio transmissions, improved asdic systems located the enemy with greater precision and radar found them on the surface. The Allies cracked the submariners' signal code, and new devices such as the 'hedgehog' - a system for throwing bombs ahead of a corvette when she made asdic contact – lengthened the odds against the Germans. Escort carriers went with the convoys and shot down the huge Condor aircraft used by the Germans to send information to the U-boats as well as to attack the convoys. Corvette crews trained intensively, and their captains learned to work together in attack groups rather than as individuals. While the pusser navy ashore stressed discipline, the volunteers learned to fight as a team in an egalitarian setting where all suffered alike. Many of the U-boat aces went down with their boats, and inexperienced commanders and crews fell prey to the improved fighting spirit and technology acquired by the Royal Canadian Navy. In May 1943, a wolf pack attacked Convoy ONS 5 and lost 21 boats. Doenitz withdrew his submarines from the North Atlantic in that month. They came back in September, equipped with acoustic torpedoes that homed in on the noise made by a ship's propellors.

Some Canadian ships gained a reputation for being happy and lucky. Such a one was the destroyer HMCS *Haida*. After taking part in the D-Day invasion, she patrolled off the western tip of Brittany, seeking out submarines leaving or returning to their bases in France. One 24 June, *Haida* raced to a spot where an RAF Liberator had depth-charged a U-boat. *Haida* dropped her depth charges and the crew promptly put pails over the side and began to scoop up herring stunned by the blasts. While so occupied, they saw the German submarine surface. The destroyer's guns opened up, shattering the hull and conning tower of U-971. Crew members also remember their return to Plymouth after this venture, with every gun trained on 'Skin Hill' – the rangefinders ensured that the sailors had a splendid view of the women sunbathing there!

Above: *A happy ship: The destroyer HMCS Haida in Plymouth, England, 4 July 1944. This photograph gives a good view of the camouflage pattern used by the ship. Such patterns were meant to 'disrupt' the outline of the ship.*

Right: *U-889 surrenders near Shelburne, Nova Scotia, after the war ended in May 1945. Note the 'snorkel' equipment on the side of the conning tower and folded down on deck. This enabled U-boats to recharge their batteries without surfacing.*

An incident on HMCS *Iroquois*, another 'Tribal' class destroyer, shows how tensions arose over minor issues. Escorting a troop convoy to Gibraltar, she helped to beat off an attack by German Focke-Wulf aircraft. Embarking survivors from the *Duchess of York* which had been set ablaze by the bombers, *Iroquois* headed for Plymouth. On the way she picked up three survivors of a sunken U-boat. In port the jacket of one of the survivors, an officer, was cleaned and returned to him – with a badge missing. Someone on the ship had 'scalped' it, and the captain demanded its return, threatening to stop all leave if it did not appear. The crew remained mute, and just before *Iroquois* sailed all those below the rank of leading hand refused duty. When informed of this the captain collapsed with a heart attack, and had to be removed from command. Common sense finally prevailed, and the crew went back to duty.

Some 'Tribal' class destroyers were notoriously unlucky. Canada lacked the resources and expertise to build these new powerful vessels. While under construction at the Vickers-Armstrong shipyard in Newcastle-on-Tyne, England, a hull received a hit from a German bomb in April 1941. Named HMCS *Athabaskan* when completed, this ship slid down the stocks in November 1941. After trials, the destroyer patrolled the gap between the Faroe Islands and Iceland where storms incessantly battered her and stressed her hull.

In the summer of 1943, *Athabaskan* fell victim to a new German weapon in the Bay of Biscay. Dornier

217 aircraft released HS293 radio-controlled glider bombs, and two of them hit the destroyer on 24 August. One passed right through the ship, but another exploded, killing five sailors and wounding two others. On fire, *Athabaskan* limped back to port.

Lt. Cdr. John Stubbs then took command, and worked hard to turn *Athabaskan* into a happy ship. The destroyer went on the Murmansk run, and to the Azores, then patrolled off northwest France with three other Tribals, including HMCS *Haida*. In a night action on 26 April 1944, the two ships set a German Fleet Torpedo Boat on fire. A few nights later they fought two German destroyers off Morlaix. A torpedo hit *Athabaskan* on the starboard side, wrecking two guns and smashing the propulsion system, leaving the ship dead in the water and on fire. *Haida* pursued one German torpedo boat, driving it on to the rocks. At 4:28 a.m. on 29 April, *Athabaskan* blew up. *Haida* stopped and scooped men from the sea as Stubbs moved among his men, telling them to sing and to keep moving. Then he told the *Haida* to leave the scene.

Bobbing on floats and in lifejackets, the sailors of the lost ship saw the destroyer pick up speed and depart. Then one of the enemy ships returned to rescue survivors. When they debarked at Brest, the captain saluted the Canadians and hoped there were

Top left: *Survivors of HMCS* Clayoquot, *sunk by a U-boat just outside Halifax Harbour on 24 December 1944.*

Left: *A Canadian minesweeper approaches Antwerp on 26 November 1944, after clearing the channel to the port.*

Above: *Families watch as HMCS* Skeena *docks at Halifax in March 1941.*

no hard feelings between them. In the following days, the bodies of 59 of the *Athabaskan*'s dead, including its captain, washed up on the coast of Finisterre. A total of 128 Canadian sailors had died.

Canadian sailors crewed landing craft taking troops ashore on D-Day and served on Motor Torpedo Boats in the English Channel and the Mediterranean, where they earned a piratical reputation. The corvettes *Prince Arthur* and *Regina* each accounted for an Italian submarine off North Africa.

The minesweeper *Guysborough* helped to clear the English Channel before D-Day. An acoustic torpedo hit her on 17 March 1945, in the Bay of Biscay. William Ingraham, at 25 one of the oldest men on the ship, recalled shaving at the time, as *Guysborough* was due to dock in England on the next day. The ship had left Canada the previous year, its asdic and radar inoperative, armed with a small gun that no one knew how to fire, with a crew that knew how to march and salute but little about operating the vessel. The first torpedo failed to sink the ship, but the second one did. Blown into the water, Ingraham attached himself to a raft crowded with numbed and shocked sailors. The engineer appeared to be in good spirits, but suddenly slumped forward, dead. Ingraham heard a sailor desperately trying to awaken a dead friend. Another shipmate, drunk on saved-up

rum, died singing in the water, dragged down by his heavy sheep's wool jacket. At 2 p.m. on the following day, a British ship picked up the 49 survivors of the ship's complement of 90.

Canada's little ships accounted for 27 U-boats, 17 of them after November 1943, and lost 24 ships and 1150 men. The country also lost 1148 merchant seamen. In all, 40,000 Germans served in U-boats; 28,000 died and 7000 were captured. The war at sea ended at 10:01 p.m. on 8 May, when the German High Command ordered all U-boats to surrender.

Attention turned to the Pacific where HMCS *Uganda*, lent by the Royal Navy to Canada, served in the war against Japan, surviving attacks by *kamikazes* (suicide pilots). In the East, the Canadian navy won its only Victoria Cross of the war. Lt. Robert Gray took part in an attack on Japanese destroyers at Onagawa on the Inland Sea. Batteries on the ships and on shore opened up as Gray dove at a destroyer. Holding his blazing plane steady, he dropped his bombs on the enemy vessel, sinking it, before plunging to his death in the bay.

The experiences of the RCN in the Second World War showed that the era of the big ships had ended, and that those who dominated the skies above the sea – and the waters beneath it – would control the oceans in the future.

The
Korean
War

> . . . by far the most important non-American contribution
> was that of Canada and other nations of the British
> Commonwealth.
> MAX HASTING, *The Korean War* (1987)

Canada came out of the Second World War with the world's third largest navy, its fourth largest air force, and 100 battle-seasoned, battalion-sized combat units in northwest Europe.

Most servicemen doffed their uniforms and returned to civvy street with a sigh of relief. 'Buzz' Beurling went to fight for the Israelis in their war of independence. He died when the engine of the plane he was flying to Palestine failed as it left Rome on 20 May 1948. His three companions perished with him – they had served in the Luftwaffe. Ben Dunkleman reached Israel, hoping to command an independent unit of Canadian volunteers. Instead, the Israelis placed the Canadian soldiers in assault groups. In July 1948, Dunkleman commanded the 7th Brigade that cleared the Arab armies out of Galilee.

Peter Worthington joined the Royal Canadian Navy in 1944 at the age of 17, and left it as a 'veteran' just before his 19th birthday in 1946, feeling he had been robbed of an opportunity to see action. At 4 a.m. on 25 June 1950, 90,000 North Korean troops crossed the 38th Parallel and swept south to conquer the divided nation. And Worthington got his chance for adventure.

Above: *Brigadier Rockingham briefs officers of the Princess Pat's in Korea, 4 October 1951.*

Left: *A machine gun team of the 25th Canadian Infantry Brigade in Korea, 25 May 1951.*

Top right: *Canadian soldiers make the most of the Korean winter, playing hockey at the 'Imjin Gardens.'*

Right: *Canadian engineers examine a Chinese box mine.*

Overleaf: *Sherman tanks of Lord Strathcona's Horse, July 1952.*

Two days after the invasion, President Harry Truman promised air and naval support to South Korea for what he called a 'police action.' On the same day the United Nation's Security Council declared that there had been a breach of the peace, and a United Nations Unified Command came into being early in July to protect South Korea, under General Douglas MacArthur. Canada sent three Tribal class destroyers to Korea, and 426 Transport Squadron of the RCAF began supply runs to the Land of Morning Calm. The American troops sent to stem the invasion fled before the North Koreans until only a small area around Pusan in the southeast remained unoccupied.

A Cabinet discussion which took place on the special train returning from Prime Minister Mackenzie King's funeral on 22 July 1950 resulted in the establishment of an expeditionary force to Korea on 7 August. On 15 September, General MacArthur landed his troops behind enemy lines at Inchon, the port of Seoul. Canadian destroyers supported the daring operation. The American 8th Army broke out of the Pusan perimeter and drove the North Koreans back over the 38th Parallel, and it looked as if the war had been won.

Then 180,000 Chinese volunteers crossed the Yalu River that divided their country from North Korea and swept down the peninsula, routing the United Nations force and their Korean allies. By this time a battalion of the Princess Patricia's Canadian Light Infantry had arrived in the country.

When the call to serve in Korea went out, all manner of men flocked to the recruiting depots. Of the first 10,000 volunteers, 30 percent deserted or had to be discharged. They included a 14-year-old boy, a 72-year-old man, and a former Japanese prisoner of war with severe medical problems.

Colonel Jim Stone, the battalion commander in Korea, made sure his men were properly trained before going into battle. On their way to the front, the Canadians passed the bodies of 68 black Americans. Thrown untrained into battle, they had not dug in for the night. The Chinese slaughtered them as they lay in their sleeping bags. After that sight, it proved difficult to get Canadian troops to use their bags.

For two years, Canada's contingent in Korea attacked and defended hills. In February the Princess Pat's lost four men killed in attacking Hill 444.

Left: *Canadian destroyers HMCS* Huron *(foreground) and* Iroquois *off Japan, 13 December 1953.*

Below: *A Bren gun crew of the Princess Pat's in winter positions, March 1951.*

Right: *Gunners of the Royal Canadian Horse Artillery shell Chinese troops attacking Little Gibraltar Hill.*

In late April, the battalion distinguished itself at Kapyong, northeast of Seoul. The Canadians advanced as the Republic of Korea's troops fell back, leaving one soldier to wonder why he was on his way up the line while the Korean soldiers went the other way. Thousands of Chinese overran a hill held by Australians, and then surged toward Hill 677, which was held by the Canadians. The Canadians, well dug in, stopped the onslaught in a confused night action, losing ten men killed and 23 wounded. Private Ken Barwise, a former sawmill worker, won the Military Medal for killing six Chinese, and the battalion received the United States Presidential Citation. In May 1951, the Royal Canadian Regiment took three hills at Chail-li near the 38th Parallel, but had to retreat later, losing six dead.

As the Korean conflict turned into a stalemate, it began to resemble the warfare on the Western Front in the First World War. The stink of death pervaded the Canadian lines in a country that baked in summer and froze in winter. The prevalent filth and poverty dismayed the troops, who shared their rations with the peasants and took care of orphaned children.

The casual brutality of life in Korea appalled the Canadians. An officer complained that a Korean soldier assigned to his platoon kept falling asleep on duty. Before anyone could intervene, a Korean officer arrived, made the soldier dig his own grave, and then had him shot.

Peter Worthington recalled the characteristic pattern of tedium and terror that marked his time with

Left: *The stress of war: Pvt Norris of the Royal Canadian Regiment awaits medical aid after a night patrol.*

Below: *Members of the Royal 22e Regiment – the 'Van Doos' – advance.*

Below right: *L/Cpl Robert Sobol of the Princess Pat's at the grave of Pvt Lloyd Wylie at the United Nations cemetery at Pusan.*

the Princess Pat's in Korea. On one patrol, his men ambushed a party of Chinese, but then found all their weapons except the Sten guns iced up and unable to fire. As the Chinese artillery opened up, the Canadians made a hasty retreat. On another occasion Worthington's men became overly relaxed and very bellicose after drinking from their canteens. The platoon sergeant had picked up containers of overproof rum, but on that night the patrol did not meet any Chinese. On Christmas Eve 1952, the Chinese left gift-bedecked trees and propaganda pamphlets in front of the Canadian lines. Worthington's men sneaked across to the Chinese lines and left behind cans of ham chunks and lima beans.

HMCS *Haida* cruised around Korea, becoming known as 'The Galloping Ghost of the Korean Coast' and firing on trains. In the summer of 1952, the RCN formed a Trainbusters' Club. To gain entry, a ship had to destroy an enemy train. On 19 December *Haida* 'severely bent' ten boxcars, then qualified for the club by destroying four trains near Yang-do on 26 May 1953.

The Royal Canadian Air Force did not participate in the air war over Korea, but Canada assigned 22 fighter pilots who flew F86 Sabre jets with the United States Fifth Air Force. Flt. Lt. J. A. O. Levesque scored the first Canadian kill, shooting down a North Korean MiG 15 on 30 March 1950, and by the time the war ended Canadians had recorded nine kills.

Sqn. Ldr. Andrew MacKenzie, who had accounted for eight planes in the Second World War, went down on his fifth sortie on 8 December 1952. Hit by an American fighter near the Yalu River, the plane went into a violent spin and MacKenzie baled out. His captors held him for two years, constantly threatening him and leaving MacKenzie in solitary confinement for weeks on end in Chinese prisons in Manchuria. 'Being locked up sure made me appreciate life in a free world,' MacKenzie said. He bore no resentment toward the pilot who shot him down: 'We all made mistakes.'

In all, 26,791 Canadians served in Korea. A total of 312 of them died in combat and another 200 in incidents associated with the war. The 'police action' ended with an armistice signed at Panmunjon on 27 July 1953, and an uneasy peace settled on the world. Canada's armed forces began to look for new roles, but received little money for new equipment. A sailor recalled the breakdowns, failures and malfunctions that dogged HMCS *Haida* in the early 1960s and lowered the morale of her crew. While chipping paint off the destroyer's deck, the tool went right through the plating!

The Korean war showed the futility of such conflicts. When the next invasion of one country by another took place, Canada played a prominent role in halting it and bringing into being a United Nations force dedicated to keeping the peace rather than fighting wars.

The Peaceful Uses of Canada's Military Forces

The grim fact is that we prepare for war like precocious
giants and for peace like retarded pygmies.
LESTER B. PEARSON, *Acceptance Speech, Nobel Peace Prize,
Oslo, Norway* (10 December 1957)

John Robert Colombo and Michael Richardson's book *We Stand on Guard for Thee*, published in 1985, contains verses celebrating the Indian Wars, the Massacre of Seven Oaks on 19 June 1816, the Fenian Raids, and the Nile Expedition of 1884, as well as the major wars in which Canadians have been involved. For the period since the Korean conflict, the editors found plenty of protest and anti-war songs, but none celebrating Canada's peacekeeping efforts. This is strange, considering that Canada invented international peacekeeping in its present form.

In late October 1956, Britain, France and Israel invaded Egypt after President Nasser nationalized the Suez Canal on 28 July. Canada refused to support Britain, and the United States objected violently to the invasion. Canada took the initiative in drafting a United Nations resolution to form a United Nations emergency international force 'to secure and supervise cessation of hostilities.' Major General E. L. M. Burns became its commander. Canada had already played a significant role in peacekeeping, sending observers to Kashmir in 1949, Palestine in 1953 and Indochina in 1954. As Canada's Minister of External Affairs, Lester B. Pearson played a key role in bringing into being the UN force and easing the invaders out of Egypt, and for this he received the Nobel Peace Prize in 1957. Canada became the first UN member to earmark a military unit for peacekeeping duties. The White Paper on Defence in 1964 stated that, 'The combined land, sea and air force normally stationed in Canada and at Canadian ports will be sufficiently flexible to satisfy almost any conceivable requirement for UN . . . operations.' On 3 April 1969, however, the new government of Pierre-Elliott Trudeau put the surveillance of Canada and the protection of sovereignty at the top of defence priorities. The last priority was 'the performance of such international peacekeeping roles as we may from time to time assume.' Canada had become a member of the North Atlantic Treaty Organization, formed in 1949 at the height of the Cold War, and also belonged to the North American Air Defence Command, which had come into being in 1958. Commitments to NATO and NORAD came before peacekeeping as Canada entered the 1970s. Yet, in October 1970, Prime Minister Trudeau invoked the War Measures Act and sent troops into the streets of Canada to counter an internal threat to Canada. Two small cells of the Quebec Liberation Front kidnapped a Quebec provincial minister and the British trade commissioner, but the federal government thought they faced an insurrection and overreacted.

After the October crisis, the Trudeau government neglected Canada's armed forces, whose morale had

been shattered by unification on 1 February 1968. During the 1970s, the combined forces suffered freezes, squeezes and cutbacks, and fell prey to every management fad in Ottawa and to every theory about future wars. Canada stayed out of the Vietnam War, but happily sold military supplies to the United States and welcomed American draft dodgers. Some 5-6000 Canadians served with the US forces in Vietnam, enlisting because they were bored or to seek glory. About 56 men died in action, including the son of Canada's former chief of defense staff and Second World War veteran, General Jacques Dextraze.

Meanwhile, Canada seemed to be losing interest in peacekeeping. Writing in 1983, Geoffrey Pearson, Lester's son and a member of the Department of External Affairs, noted that even by 1970 'the image of Canada as a "helpful fixer" was wearing thin.'

Above: *Prime Minister Mackenzie King at the founding meeting of the United Nations.*

Right: *A Canadian soldier in winter gear.*

In the 1980s, the high cost of new war technology at a time of rising government deficits led to cutbacks in military spending. Routinization and bureaucratization created rigidity at a time when combat demanded great flexibility. A survey in 1988 revealed that Canada had 16.2 generals or admirals for every 10,000 troops, compared to 4.9 for the United States for the same number.

In 1989, the federal government cancelled plans to spend $8 billion on nuclear-powered submarines. Canada decided it could 'protect' its Arctic with three surveillance planes and sea floor sensors. The 1989 budget also will result in the closing of 14 military bases and a saving of $5.7 billion in defence costs over the next five years.

Meanwhile, NATO, faced with uncertainty about its role as the Soviet Union became more concerned with internal tensions than with external threats, came in for criticism. In Labrador, the Innu protested plans for turning their land into a NATO weapons training centre. In the fall of 1988, a German farmer, angered like the Innu by low-flying planes, sprayed a Canadian tank on manoeuvres with liquid manure.

The controversy over the budget cuts and the role and value of NATO and NORAD has masked the excellent work being done by Canada's armed forces in serving the national and international community. Since 1956, Canadians have helped to keep the peace in Egypt, Lebanon, Zaire, West Irian, Yemen, Cyprus, the Dominican Republic, Nigeria, Syria, Afghanistan and Iran-Iraq. In 1989, Canadian troops went to Namibia to keep the peace between warring factions there. As one soldier put it, peacekeeping is 'boring and frustrating, and sometimes it's dangerous.' In Lebanon, Canadian peacekeepers have had their vehicles hijacked, their apartments wrecked, and have been threatened with death.

In 1988, the Nobel Peace Prize went to the UN Peacekeeping Force. Cpl. Jeff Docksey of Strathcona's Horse represented Canada at the award ceremony in Oslo. By 1988, 80,000 Canadian soldiers had been peacekeepers, and 81 of them had died in the course of their duties. The UN is experiencing

difficulty in finding funds for peacekeeping. The expected cost of this effort in 1989, $1.5 billion (US), however, is only one percent of the value of the world's arms exports in 1987.

In 1910, William James' *The Moral Equivalent of War* appeared, claiming that, 'War is the strong life, it is life *in extremis*.' James saw the central issue of his time as 'one of turning the individual and collective heroism and sacrifice demanded by war into more constructive channels.' Canada's armed forces are trying to do this. In 1957-58, they provided support for 'Operation Hazen,' a scientific expedition that formed part of Canada's contribution to the International Geophysical Year. Canada co-operates with the United States, the Soviet Union, France, Norway and Britain in a search and rescue system called SARSAT, in which satellites pinpoint trans-

missions from downed planes and sinking ships. The armed forces have an excellent record in search and rescue throughout Canada. In December 1983, a helicopter-destroyer ploughed through the roaring darkness of the North Atlantic to rescue the crew of Panamanian bulk freighter *Ho Ming 5*. One sailor on HMCS *Iroquois* removed a stunned fish from the port bridge nine metres above the heaving seas as the Canadian sailors and the Korean freighter crew confronted a common enemy – wild nature.

Canada's armed forces have fought fires in national parks; dealt with disastrous floods in the Fraser Valley and Winnipeg; flown food to starving people in Africa; assisted Jamaicans in cleaning up after the hurricane in 1988; and delivered building supplies to Indian communities in northern Ontario. In 1989, Canadian forces' transport planes flew people out of remote communities and Indian villages threatened by fire in Ontario and Manitoba.

Far left: *Two members of the Queen's Own Rifles leave Calgary in November 1956, to join the United Nations Peacekeeping Force in Egypt.*

Right: *Troops of the Canadian Airborne Regiment drop from a Hercules, somewhere in the Canadian Arctic.*

Above: *Members of the Royal Canadian Dragoons leave the Gaza Strip between Israel and Egypt in February 1960 after serving a year with the United Nations Emergency Force.*

Above and left: *The new look of land warfare: Canadian troops equipped to fight in winter.*

Top right: *Canadian paratroopers and a Chinook helicopter.*

Right: *Members of Canada's Airborne Regiment fire a General Purpose Machine Gun.*

Above: *Members of the Royal Canadian Dragoons in a Leopard tank. The German-made Leopard I was one of the* *principal NATO main battle tanks in the 1970s and 1980s but is now being replaced.* Below: *Special Service Force troops take part in a mock battle. Canadian, British and other NATO forces regularly use the* *wide-open spaces of Canada's prairies for a variety of training manoeuvres.*

Above: *A C-130 Hercules delivers supplies via LAPES – Low Altitude Parachute Extraction System.*

Left: *The Special Service Force, an elite group, shown here on manoeuvres.*

Far left: *A Canadian Leopard Bridge Layer moves out of woods during a NATO exercise in West Germany.*

Left: *Canadian Forces submarine HMCS Okanagan in St John's Harbour, Newfoundland.*

Above: *A Canadian destroyer in Windsor, Ontario.*

Right: *A Canadian submarine in Halifax Harbour.*

Above: *Canadian naval ships in the port of Vancouver.*

Left: *A Canadian destroyer at sea.*

Top right: *Canadair's Sabre V, now obsolete.*

Right: *The Canadian Snowbird Team.*

Left: *A Northrop CF-5D.*

Right: *A CF-104 Starfighter.*

Below: *The former RCAF aerobatics team the Golden Hawks was composed of F86-Ds.*

While the services explore new roles, a group of veterans has begun to promote peace and disarmament and to encourage the search for the moral equivalent of war. C. G. 'Giff' Gifford of Halifax completed 49 missions as a Pathfinder with the RCAF and won the Distinguished Flying Cross. 'We were proud to be Pathfinders,' he says. 'We were scared every time we took off – it was nerve-wracking.' As navigator in the master bomber, Gifford remained over the target for 20 minutes on some missions. 'In one sense, we took more risks than the other crews. But we were proud that we mastered the necessary skills – and survived,' he observes.

Gifford has become a Pathfinder for peace now. Worried about the breakdown in detente between the Russians and Americans in the late 1970s, he founded Veterans Against Nuclear Arms (VANA) with three others in 1982. He is now Chairman of VANA, which has 14 branches across Canada, and is executive director of the Defence Research and Education Centre. Concern with defence has created a small industry of conferences, seminars

Left: *In an eerie red glow, a Canadian fighter pilot controls a multi-million dollar, high-tech killing machine.*

Below left: *An F-101 Voodoo of 425 Squadron.*

and academic research around such topics at the 'high-intensity battlefield.' Gifford points out that most military pay little attention to the fact that nuclear weapons have changed the ground rules of war forever. In the Second World War, major cities became battlefields, and civilians died in their thousands. In 1988 alone, 22 wars killed 416,000 people. Ethnic strife, rebellions from the right and left, power struggles between rival religious factions, clashes over territory, and struggles for 'independence' caused most of the wars. The majority of those killed were civilians – not soldiers.

Until recently, many Canadian veterans shut up their feelings about having been in combat. 'The "tough guy" attitude of some serves to suppress their feelings,' says Gifford. 'So much grief, not guilt, grief for the things that happened that one wishes had not happened lurks underneath. 'A Canadian fighter pilot shot up a vehicle in France after D-Day, killing the driver as he sought safety in a ditch. Then he saw he had attacked a farmer's cart. Until recently he had not told his family about the incident. When he did, he cried.

Below: A Canadian Armed Forces, CT-114 training aircraft. These aircraft entered service with the then RCAF in 1965 and, as well as for their normal duties, have been used by the 'Snow Bird' aerobatic team.

A member of VANA, now a judge in Victoria, flew Wellington bombers in Malta, receiving orders to kill downed enemy aircrew in the Mediterranean. Shot down in 1942, the plane's crew bobbed around in a dinghy for three days. Then a German plane flew over, and they thought, 'This is it!' The Ju 88 circled twice and flew away. On the following day, the Canadians' base received a signal from the Red Cross in Rome, giving their location. 'When the judge talks to schoolchildren, he tells them that a German saved his life,' Gifford says.

When he began to promote peace and disarmament, Gifford felt as scared as he did when he started flying missions. 'I had some of the same feelings as when I became a Pathfinder – of sticking my neck out, of going against the tide,' he recalls. 'But I felt it was necessary to do it. Now the tide of battle has turned, and we have a strong feeling that the majority of Canadians are with us.' He sees a need to reorient the military from concern with killing to relieving misery and suffering in disaster relief, and promoting national and international development. 'The navy's already committed to this, in assisting the Coast Guard,' he points out. 'So is the air force, through Air Transport Command. The army needs clarity, dignity and public support, and a peaceful role in development would ensure this.' Idealism and the quest for adventure mark Canada's youth as it does all others. And 'Giff' Gifford believes that service with Canada's armed forces in peaceful and developmental pursuits could provide the motivation for the country's young people as war once did.

The experiences and words of one VANA member show how compassion and humanity can triumph in the worst conditions. Herman Campbell, who died in the mid-1980s, won the Military Medal for taking a German machine gun post. He had joined up at 16, and enjoyed the rigorous life while training in Canada and at Aldershot. When he reached the war zone, Campbell found that 'destruction, not upbuilding, was the aim.' As he heard the big guns, he realized he was potential cannon fodder. But he survived the miseries of trench life. Wounded in the head on 8 August 1918 in the Battle of Amiens, Campbell staggered to the dressing station. Then, from a heap of rubble, he heard 'a sound of pleading groans.' He located a wounded German soldier 'seeking my compassion and the strength to assist him.' Campbell took the German on his shoulders and staggered on. Campbell recalled, 'Our blood mingled even as did our thoughts, and we exchanged the identical view that we were not personal enemies, but caught up in a hellish pursuit which should have no place in human society - that war, itself, is the great enemy of mankind.'

In his poem, 'In Flanders Field,' John McRae, writing near a war cemetery, demanded on behalf of the dead that others 'Take up our quarrel with the foe . . . . ' And as the experiences of 'Giff' Gifford, Hubert Campbell and thousands of others who fought at the sharp end show, the foe is not other human beings – it is war itself, and the hatreds and fears that lead to it.

INDEX

Page numbers in italics refer to illustrations

Acadia, 11, 12
Admiral Scheer, 154
Afrika Corps, 110, 141
Alaunia, HMS, 155
Alcazar, *87*
Alderson, Lt.Gen. Edwin, 27, 37
Aleutians, 131, 137
Anderson, Maj. Peter, 66
Andree Dupre, HMCS, *154-55*, 155
Anzio, 118, 137
Arnhem, 129, 137
Assiniboine, HMCS, *152*, 157, *158*
Athabaskan, HMCS, 158, 160
Atlantic, Battle of the, 153, 157

Bader, S/L Douglas, 139, 140
Barker, Maj. William George, 74, 75, *75*, 78, 79, 148
Belgium, 24, 41, 49, 70, 98, 139
Berlin, Battle of, 136, 146
Bernard, Jack, *97*
Bernard, Warren, *97*
Bethune, Dr. Norman, 90, *90*
Beurling, George 'Buzz', 141, *141*, 142, 150, 164
Bird, Will R., 28, 31, 55, 56, 57, 58, 59, 61, 65, 66
Bishop, William Avery, 72, *72*, 73, *73*, 74, 78, 79, 101, 103, 136, 141, 148
black soldiers, 31, 168
Boers, 19, 21
Bolsheviks, 61, 66, 78
Borden, P.M. Sir Robert, 27, 58, *58*, 59, 60, 62, 63, 66
Boulton, Maj.Gen. C., 17, 19
Boyle, Lt.Col. Russell, 27, 28
Brillant, Lt. Jean, 63
Britain, 12, 13, 24, 100, 144, 146, 174
Britain, Battle of, 136, *136*, 140
British troops, 27, 28, 35, 38, 42, 49, 98, 101, 117, 121, 122
Brooke, Margaret, 157
Brookwood Cemetery, *108*
Brophy, John B. 'Don', 75, 76, 79
Brutinel, Raymond, 29, 31, 37
Buchanan, James, 42, 44
Burns, Maj.Gen. E.L.M., 35, 174
Bury, SS, *154*

Cadbrook, L.H., *145*
Calgary Regiment, 105, 108
Cambrai, 40, 65
Camp Borden, Ontario, *70, 77*
Canada, HMCS, 80
Canada's 1st Army, *26-7*
Canada's Hundred Days, 48, 63, 65, 66
Canadian Air Regiment, *177, 179*
Canadian Cartridge Co., 57
Canadian Corps, 37, *38-9*, 41, 42, 47, 48, 61, 62, 63, 65, 99
Canadian Engineers, 119, *165*
Canadian Expeditionary Forces (CEF), 25, 31, 66, 69, 70, 73, 74, *81*

Canadian Light Horse, 65, *65*
Canadian Motor Machine Gun Brigade (1st), 29, 31
Canadian Pacific RR, *19, 100-01*
Canadian 2nd Division, 77, *98*
Canadian Snowbird team, *7, 185*
Canadian Women's Army Corps, 98, *134*
Cape Breton Highlanders, *120*, 121
Carleton and York Regiment, 115, 119
casualties, 32, 40, 41, *41*, 54, 58, 61, 63, 65, 66, 115, 119, 121, 122, 126, 130, 131, 132, 135, 136, 140, 146, 153, 155, 156, 157, 158, 161, 171, 174, 189
Charlottetown, HMCS, 157
Chatham, SS, 157
Churchill, P.M. Winston, 6, 99, *99*, *105*
Collins, Robert, 150, 151
Collishaw, Maj. Raymond, 72, *74*, 78, 148
Constitution, USS, *15*
convoys, *153*, 153, 157, 158
corvettes, 155, 156, *157*, 158, 161
Crerar, Gen. Harry, 110, 135
Currie, Gen. Arthur, *21, 32*, 32, 35, 42, 48, *48*, 49, 50, 58, 61, 62, *62*, 63, *64*, 65, 66, *128*
Currie, Maj. David, 127, 135
Curtiss, JN-4, *75*

D-Day, 108, 122, *122, 123*, 125, 156, 158, 161
map, *124-25*
Death of General Wolfe, *14*
Decatsye, Pvt. L.R., *129*
Dieppe, 104, *104*, 105, *105*, 108, 150
D.F.C., 137, 140, 141, 142, 188
D.S.O., 74, 103, 119, 132, 141, 142
Doenitz, Adm. Karl, 153, 158
Donald Stewart, SS, 157
Dorniers, 139, 140, 158, 160, 161
Douai, 44, 65
Duchess of York, SS, 158
Dunkirk, 98, 139, 152, 153
Dunkleman, Ben, 122, 125, 129, 132, 164
Dunphy, Rod, 136, 148

Edmonton Highlanders, 117, 119
8th Army, 112, 118
English explorers, *10-11*, 12
Essex Scottish Regiment, 105, 134
Ewen, Jean, 90, 91

F86-D Sabre Jets, 171, *187*
Festubert, 32, 35
5th Canadian Armoured Brigade, *121*
5th Division, *34*
Fighter Command Base, *139*
1st Brigade, 117, 119, 139
1st Canadian Division, *25*, 35, 37, 94, 112, 134
1st Canadian Infantry Division, 115, 117, 118, 119
1st Canadian Parachute Battalion, 122, 134
1st Hussars, *124*
Flanders, 24, 28, 29, *49*, 50, 61
Focke-Wulfe Fw 190, 141, 158
Fort Cataraqui, SS, 130

Fort Louisbourg, 12, 13, *13, 14*
Foster, Maj.Gen. Harry, 94, 127
France, 12, 13, 24-66, 122, 139, 142, 144, 150, 160, 174
Franco, Gen. Francisco, 86, *87*
Fraser, HMCS, 153
French infantryman (1659), *11*
Fumerton, W/C 'Moose', DFC, *149*

Galloway, Strome, 117, 119
Garner, Hugh, 86, 90, 91
gas warfare, 32, *33*
Gatling gun, *18*
George, P.M. Lloyd, 40, 41, 68
German Condor Legion, *86*
German troops, *106-07*
Germany, 24-66, 94, 104, 112, 119, 129, 132, 134, 140, 146, 150, 153
Ghosts Have Warm Hands, 28, 48
Gifford, C.G. 'Giff', 188, 189
Godefroy,Hugh, *145*
'Golden Hawks', *187*
Good Hope, HMS, 80
Gregory, Maj. R.A., 122, 132
Grilse, HMCS, 80
Guerriere, HMS, *15*
Gustav Line, *112*, 117, 118
Guysborough, HMCS, 161

Haida, HMCS, *158*, 158, 160, 171
Haig, Gen. Douglas, 48, 49, 50, 62
Halifaxes, 146, *147*, 150
Hampdens, 144, 150
Harris, Sir Arthur 'Bomber', 144, 145, 148
Harrison, Charles, 62, 63
Hartwig, Lt.Cdr. Paul, 157
Hastings and Prince Edward Regiment, 'Hasty Pees', *110*, 112, 115, 117, 118
Hees, Maj. George, 130, 135
Hercules, *177, 180-81*
Hickson, Arthur, 54, 55
Hitler, Adolph, 86, 110, 154
Hitler Line, 118, 119
Hochelaga, HMCS, 80
Holland, 98, 129, *130*, 134, 135
Ho Ming 5, SS, 176
Hong Kong, 99, 100, *100*, 103
howitzer, *34-5, 36-7*
Hughes, Col. Sam, *25*, 25, 27, 69
Huron, HMCS, *168*
Hurricanes, 137, *138*, 139, *141, 142-43*

Iceland, 98, 144
Imo, 82-3
Indians, 10-19
In Flanders Field, 189
International Brigade, 16, 86, *88*, 91
Inuit, *10-11*, 10, 11
Iroquois, HMCS, 158, *168*, 176
Iroquois, 10, 11, 12
Israel, 164, 174
Italy, 35, 110-21
map, *119*

Japan, 90, 91, 99, *100*, 101, 103, 131, 137,

140, 161
Jervis Bay, SS, 154
King, P.M. William Lyon Mackenzie, 6, 99, *99*, 103, 131, *131*, *135*, 165, *174*
King George V, 29, 31
King George VI, 94
Korean War, 6, 164-171

Lancasters, 144, *144*, 146, 148, 150
Lancaster to Berlin, 136
Laurier, P.M. Sir Wilfrid, 19, *20*, 24, 25, *59*, *80*
Lawrence, Hal, 155, 156, 157
Lawson, Brig-Gen. J.K., 100, 101, 103
Le Brun, Pvt. Ronald, 54, *55*
Leipzig, 80
Leopard tank, *180*
Les Fusiliers Mont-Royal, 108
Levis, HMCS, 155
liberators, 137, 157, 158
'Llandovery Castle', 63
Luftwaffe, 141, 164
Lundy's Lane, Battle of, 15
Lunenburg, HMCS, *155*
Lysanders, *137*

MacBrien, Gen., *48*
MacDonald, P/O Peter, 137, 139
McEwen, 'Black Mike', 146
McIntyre, Commander, 56, 57
MacKenzie, Lt. Hugh, 52
MacKenzie, S/L Andrew, 171
MacKenzie, William Lyon, 15
McKnight, F/O Willie, 140
McLeod, S/L Wally, 141, 142, *142*
McNab, S/L E.A., 139, *139*, 140
McNair, W/C 'Buck', *149*
McNaughton, Brig.-Gen. 'Andy', *32*, *42*, *50*, *62*, 63, 98
'Mac-Paps'. *See* International Brigade.
MacPhee, Murdock, 52, 63, 65, 66
Malta Spitfire, 141
Messerschmitt 109, 140, 142
Messerschmitt 410, 148
Métis, 17, 19
Meyer, Gen. Kurt, 122, 125, 127
Military cross, 74, 130
Military medal, 31, 32, 169, 189
Mohawks, 11, 12
Mont Blanc, SS, 80, *82-3*, 83
Montgomery, Fld. Mar. Bernard, 49, 112, *112*, 129, 135
Montreal, 11, 15, 16
Moose Jaw, HMCS, 155, 157
Moral Equivalent of War, The, 176
Morton, Cpl. J.E., 117, 118
Mosquitoes, *145*, *149*, 150
Mowat, Farley, 115, 118
Murray, Gen. James, *12*
Mynarski, P/O Andy, 144

National Film Board, *95*
Nationalists, 86, *89*
NATO, 174, 176
Newfoundland, 12, 40, 41

Newfoundland Regiment, 38, 40, 41
Niagara Peninsula, 13, 15
Nieuport Scout, 73, *73*
9th Canadian Infantry Division, *123*
Niobe, 80, 83
NORAD, 174, 176
Normandy, 122, *122*, 125, *125*, 126, 127, 150
North Atlantic Run, 152
Northrop CF-50, *186*
Nova Scotia Rifles, 31, 61

Oakville, HMCS, 156
Okanagan, HMCS, *182*
'Operation Jubilee', 104, 105, 108
'Operation Market Garden', 129
Order of the British Empire, 137, 157
Ottawa, 15, 17, 19

Panzers, 110, 122, 125
Papineau, Louis-Joseph, 15, 16
Passchendaele, 31, 32, 48, 49, 50, *50-51*, 52, 54, *54*, 55, *55*, 57
Pathfinders, 136, 137, 148, 188, 189
Peace Tower, *6*, 6
Pearson, P.M. Lester, *71*, 174
Peden, Murray, 146, 148, 151
Pegahmagabow, Pvt.F., 31, 32
Pepperell, Gen. William, *12*
Pictou, HMCS, *156*
pillboxes, 49, 52, 56, 57, 65, 119, *125*
Price, Harold W., 76, 77
Prince David, HMCS, *122*
Princess Patricia's Canadian Light Infantry, 'Princess Pat's', 28, 32, 37, 52, 54, 65, 94, 112, *114*, 132, *164*, 168, 169, *169*, 171
Prouse, Bob, 104, 108

Quebec Liberation Front, 174, 176
Queen's Own Rifles, 122, 125, 130, 132, *176*

Rainbow, HMCS, 80, 83
Regiment de Mont Royal, *132*
Regina Rifles, 122, *124*, 125, 129
Remembrance Day, *6-7*, 6, 24
'Republicans', 86, *88*
Richelieu Valley, 13, 15
Riel, Louis, *16*, 17, 19
Road Past Vimy, The, 42
Rockingham, Brigadier, *164*
Rommel, Gen. Irwin, 110, 141
Roome, Reg, 77, 78
Ross rifle, 25, 27, 66, 98
Royal Air Force (RAF), 77, 78, 130, 137, 139, 144, 145, 148, 158
Royal Canadian Air Force (RCAF) 75, *78-9*, *79*, *98*, 136, 137, 139, 140, 141, 142, 144, 146, 150, 151, 165, 171, 188
Royal Canadian Artillery, *17*, 91, *131*
Royal Canadian Dragoons, *176*, *180*
Royal Canadian Horse Artillery, 99, *169*
Royal Canadian Navy, 80, 152, 154, 155, 157, 158, 161, 164, 171
Royal Canadian Regiment, 17, 21, 31, 105, 110, 112, 115, 117, 119
Royal Canadian Naval Volunteer Service,

153, 154, 157
Royal Flying Corps (RFC), 69, 70, 73, 74, 76, 77, 78
Royal Highlanders of Canada (Black Watch), 28, 29, 58, 126, 129, 130
Royal Naval Air Service (RNAS), 69, 70, 77
Royal Navy, 80, 161
Royal Rifles of Canada, 100, 101, 103
Royal Winnipeg Rifles, *124*
Russia, 6, 66, 78, 108, 110, 156

Sabre V (F-96), *185*
St. Laurent, Louis, *135*
Salaberry, de, C.M., 13, 15, 17
Salisbury Plain, *26*, 27
Sanctuary Wood, *31*
Saskatoon Light Infantry, *118*
School of Gunnery, 68-9
Seaforth Highlanders, 52, 117, 119
2nd Canadian Infantry Division, 129, 130
7th Canadian Infantry Brigade, *127*
Shanghai, *91*
Sherman tanks, *113*, 116-17, 122, 125, *133*, 166-67
Sioux, HMCS, 156
16th Canadian Machine Gun, 54, *55*
Skeena, HMCS, *161*
Sobol, L/Cpl Robert, *171*
Somme, Battle of the, 37, *38-9*, 38, 40, 41, 76
Sopwith Dolphins, 78-9
Spanish Civil War, 16, 86, 90, 91
Spitfires, 142, 150
Squadron, 214, 148, 151
Squadron, 242, 137, 139, 140
Squadron, 402, 142-43
Starfighter CF-104, *187*
Stirlings, 146, 148
Stranraers, *138*
Strathcona's Horse, 94, 119, 176
Stubbs, Lt.Cdr. John, 157, 160
tanks, *50*, *106-07*, *124*, *128*
tank warfare, 110, 117, 118, 119, 122, 125, 132
3rd Canadian Division, 37, 122, *126-27*
Thompson, Walter, 136, 148, 150
Tiger Moths, 141, *143*
Tuna, HMCS, 80
12th S.S. Panzers, 122, 125, 127
25th Canadian Infantry Brigade, *164*
29th Infantry Battalion, *45*
22nd Battalion, *53*
22nd (Van Doos) Regiment, 59, 98, 117, *171*
Typhoons, 121, 150, *151*

U-boats, 48, 49, 63, 80, 137, 144, *152*, 153, 154, 156, 157, 158, *159*, 161
Uganda, HMCS, 161
United States, 78, 100, 153, 155, 174

V-1 Rocket, 148, 150
Valcartier Camp, 25, *27*
Vanier, Georges, 59, 60, 61
VE Day, *134-35*
Victoria Cross, 19, 21, 25, 32, 52, 63, 65, 73,

74, 75, 79, 103, 105, 108, 117, 119, 121,
127, 132, 134, 135, 144, 161
Vietnam War, 174, 176
Viking settlement, *10*
Vimy Ridge, 31, 42, *43*, 44, *45*, *46*, 47, 58,
61
Vimy Ridge Memorial, *2-3*, *47*, *96*
Voodoo F-101, *188*

War Memorial, Ottawa, *7*
Waturus, 82
Wellingtons, 144, 146, *146-47*, 148, 189
Western Front, 27, 38, 41, 42, 49, 55, 66
Westminster Regiment, 119, 121
West Nova Scotia Regiment, 110, 119
White, Pvt. M.D., *112*
Wilkie, Agnes, 157
Williams, Lt.Gen. W., 16, 17
Winnipeg Grenadiers, 100, 101, 103
Winter Line, 117, 119
Wolfe, James, 13, *14*
Women's Auxiliary Air Force, 148
World War, First, 6, 21, 24-66, 148
    at sea, 80, 83
    in the air, 68-79
World War, Second, 6, 94-135
    at sea, 152-61
    in the air, 136-51
Worthington, Peter, 164, 169, 171
Wylie, Pvt. Lloyd, *171*

Ypres, 28, 29, 31, 32, 35, 48, 54, 78

SOURCES

This book has done no more than skim the surface of Canada's extensive military history. The best account of this field is Desmond Morton's *A Military History of Canada* (1985). With J L Granastein, Morton produced two books in 1989 on Canada's role in the First and Second World Wars – *Marching to Armageddon* and *A Nation Forged in Fire.*

Canadian writers have produced some classics of writing about life at the 'sharp end' of war, notably Will R Bird in *Ghosts Have Warm Hands* and Murray Peden in *A Thousand Shall Fall.* Morton's military history contains a very full bibliography, and readers are referred to this and to the books mentioned in the text for a fuller appreciation of how Canadians have served – and suffered – in war. Tony Foster's *A Meeting of Generals* (1986) is outstanding in conveying what the Second World War looked like through both Canadian *and* German eyes.

ACKNOWLEDGMENTS

The author and publishers wish to thank the following people for their assistance: Murray Peden, QC; CG 'Giff' Gifford; Cpl Annette Lotz; Lt Cdr Len Canfield; Commander (Rt'd) Robert A Willson (HMCS *Haida*); Capt Marsha Dorge (Editor, *Sentinel*) and her secretary Mary Boyd; David A Brigham (Dept of Veterans Benefits, Washington); Marla Hillier (Canada Post Corp); H Clifford Chadderton (The War Amputations of Canada); Lt Col Georges Boulanger (Dept of External Affairs); H A Halliday (Canadian War Museum); Norman Hillmer (National Defence Headquarters); Jean Chiaramonte Martin, the editor; Adrian Hodgkins, the designer; Rita Longabucco, the picture editor; and Elizabeth A McCarthy, the indexer.

PICTURE CREDITS

All illustrations are courtesy of The National Archives of Canada except the following:

Chas Bowyer: 78-79.
British Museum, London: 10-11(top).
Brompton Photo Library: 11(top), 72, 73, 86, 87(both), 88(both), 89(both), 91, 136, 144.
Canadian Forces Photographic Unit: 74, 139(top), 141(both), 142(top), 142-143, 145(both), 146-147(both), 149(all three), 150-151.
Canadian National Defence Department: 7(top right), 175, 177, 178(both), 179(bottom), 180-181(all five), 185(bottom).
Canadian Pacific Corporate Archives: 19.
City of Toronto Archives: 82-83.
Glenbow Archives, Calgary, Alberta: 16(bottom).
Government of Newfoundland and Labrador, Department of Tourism, Recreation and Culture: 10(bottom).
Imperial War Museum, London: 139(bottom), 140.
Library of Congress: 12(top).
National Gallery of Canada, Ottawa: 14(bottom).
National Portrait Gallery, London: 12(bottom).
Richard Natkiel: 49, 100(left), 105, 112, 119, 124-125(bottom).
New York Public Library, Rare Book Division: 11(bottom).
Nova Scotia Department of Tourism: 14(top).
The Stock Market: Cosmo Condina 6, 182-183(top); Dykstra Photos 7(bottom right), 189; Gary Fieghen 184(top); Greg Locke 182; Bill Marsh 179(top), 184(bottom), 185(top), 186, 187(top), 188(both); Bruce Rutherford 6-7(top centre); Robert Semeniuk 6-7(bottom centre); Stephen R Swan 183(bottom); Derek Trask 187(bottom).
United Nations: 174, 176(right).
US Naval Academy: 15.
US Navy: 13.
WW: 99(top), 100-101, 108, 137(all three), 138(both), 156(top), 176(left).